MARCO PEREZ was born in Vipiteno (1969), where he took over the family restaurant "Helene." After attending the Merano and Bressanone hotel school, he trained both in Italy and abroad, working with Gualtiero Marchesi and Chef Alaimo at the "Le Calandre" in Padova, among others. At the "Etoile" school in Chioggia he learned various innovative techniques that he then recreates in his recipes.

A creative chef par excellence, Perez enjoys revisiting the flavors of classic cuisine, reinterpreting them in modern and innovative versions, paying special attention to the quality of his ingredients and a healthy diet. This principle was the inspiration behind using yogurt as a primary ingredient in his creations.

YOGURT

The Italian Way to Light, Delicious Cooking

■ MARCO PEREZ ■

Photographs by Nicoletta Innocenti

CUCINA
la dolce vita
ITALIA

TIDE-MARK

Special and heartfelt thanks to my teacher Silvano Codogno for having taught me and for passing on a passion for the art of fine cuisine; to my son Ludovico and my partner Paola for the renewed energy that they have given and continue to give me; to my family for their moral support during the creation of this book, and especially to my sister, Simona, and my brother, Peter; and to my friends for having urged me to do this book.

Marco Perez

Literary and artistic copyright © Edizioni Gribaudo

Published in North America by Tide-mark Press, Ltd.
Windsor, CT

All rights in Italy and abroad, including translation, electronic storage, reproduction, adaptation, in whole or in part and by any means, are reserved for all countries and may not be granted to third parties.

First North American edition 2004

Library of Congress Control Number: 2003113663
ISBN 1-55949-9478

Editorial control and texts	MARIO BUSSO
Wine selection and coordination	CARLO VISCHI
Cover and recipe photography	NICOLETTA INNOCENTI
Project manager	VALERIO COSTANZIA
Graphic design	FEDERICO CARLO PEVERADA
Photocomposition and photolithography	GI.MAC – SAVIGLIANO (CUNEO)

All recipes were prepared by MARCO PEREZ

Printed in Korea

Contents

Aperitifs

Appetizers

Soups

First Courses

Second Courses

Yogurt and Aphrodite

by Mario Busso

Yogurt around the World

by Chiara Busso

The Land of Yogurt

by Carlo Vischi

The Unfailing Appeal of Eating Light

by Mario Busso and Carlo Vischi

The dietary wars often end in confused tangles of words, and on the battlefield the various armies fly the flags of fanatical adhesion to the religions of whole food, natural, vegetarian, macrobiotic, and on and on … Many followers do not distinguish the meaning of their credo from those of the others, because each faith tacitly implies and defers to precise precepts. But every time, the victim is pleasure, and ruling the day we find that obscurantist asceticism that defers to the consumer models dictated by fashion. There is no guidebook that fails to develop spiritual principles into ironclad rules, within whose maxims the shrewd gurus of the various brands of industrialized, mass media wisdom invite us to adopt Krishna diets rather than Ohsawa or Zen. Manuals for healthy living with healthy foods replace the delightful dark stocks and good sauces of tradition with tamari (soy sauce) and "eubiotic" waters flavored with nothing as seasonings.

There is something pathetic and infantile about these excesses. In practice they become treacherous and foolish, because in those who follow them with mystical fanaticism that healthy ambition to hedonism and pleasure without which life and the culture of well-being lose their meaning is subverted, and paradoxically, disease takes shape. Cooking that cares for human nature must, of course, replace harmful ingredients, or those that are superfluous to our energy needs, with revived foods that fit our behaviors and new requirements. But it cannot be abstracted into a sacrifice that restricts the essence of well-being to frustrating practices that lead to abstinence and the malaise it causes.

The Italian Way to Light, Delicious Cooking attempts, with light and nutritious food that is natural and versatile, to repair the conflict between the theoretical excesses and dietary weaknesses of intolerant hucksters on one side, and those on the other side who seek in food the elements of physical and spiritual pleasure and well-being. Yogurt can reestablish a balance without subjecting one to impractical and senseless sacrifices.

Yogurt, used in combination with vegetables and meats, fruits and starchy foods, shows that another type of cuisine is possible—one that balances proportions between the various elements that must compose our daily diet. This is because diet is the foundation for maintaining the best possible physical and mental conditions for the human body. The rule of proportion, moderation, *and variety of the ingredients that make up our diet is the starting point in a proper approach to ensure that vitamins, proteins, carbohydrates, fats, calcium, and acids are in balance.*

Yogurt occupies an important place in the food chain, and is practically irreplaceable (if not by milk itself) in terms of satisfying our daily need for the calcium that is indispensable to our bodies. Used with knowing skill with other ingredients, it becomes a star in the kitchen and makes possible recipes of unparalleled flavor. Marco Perez, the talented creative chef of the restaurant "Helene" in Vipiteno has created these recipes to share with you. His task is to seduce us with the "taste" that, as the gastronome Brillat-Savarin said, "Is the sense that brings us the greatest number of pleasures.... Because the pleasures of the table belong to all ages, to all conditions, to all countries and to every day; they can be associated with all the other pleasures and remain the last to console us for the loss of the rest."

From the Dawn of Time

by Flavio Boraso

Foods, and more generally the dietary process, have no history, if by history we mean that they can be written by evaluating material data and documents and interpreting them. This is the typical situation in which we find ourselves when trying to recreate the origins of fermented milk products (and therefore of yogurt), which are more similar to an ancient prehistoric civilization whose story stretches back to the dawn of time, rather than a food with a historic origin. Substantiating this assertion are the profound and basic interrelations of this food with the microscopic world of bacteria and yeasts, considered to be among the first living things appearing on the Earth millions of years ago.

Starting off down this path back in time, we are surprised once again by how dietary habits and the smallest everyday discoveries (although today we remember only fire, the wheel …) have marked our evolution to a much greater degree than we may suspect, and we can justifiably speak of a true dietary-anthropological thread that is closely tied to human anthropology. Even though we must rely on the signposts of evolution—precisely because of the absence of "reliable" documents—we can still sustain that fermented milk products (of which yogurt today is the progenitor) have had a substantial impact on the shaping and reshaping of human development through the ages, through genetic modifications.

Consider one indisputable fact: human beings are predisposed to digest milk, and mother's milk in particular, thanks to a series of enzymes that are programmed to be active only during the natural nursing period. After this period, humans should lose the capacity to "digest" lactose, thereby becoming intolerant to it, with a consequent withdrawal from the most basic food.

Today, by studying the signs left behind through the ages, we can argue that the genetic variation of "lactose tolerance" developed in certain populations of Eurasia during the Bronze Age, thanks precisely to the spread of fermented milk products. In fact, the fermentation of the milk before ingestion (transformation of the lactose into a lactic acid) overcomes most of the problems associated with intolerance. The repeated use of this "modified milk" therefore favored a positive genetic mutation, inducing a tolerance to the consumption of whole milk, and therefore favoring its reintegration into the daily diet of adults.

Almost paradoxically, these "lactophile" populations also appear to have been the most favored in the evolutionary process; not so much because of issues directly related to the consumption of this food, but rather because the animals used in the production of milk were also raised and used as pack animals, offering enormous agricultural advantages. Vice versa, and perhaps for the opposite reason, the cart and plough were unknown by the "lactophobe" populations of the Americas, and were introduced only in the pre-Columbian era. Certainly the production of milk—and its consumption and eventual transformation—is connected with the domestication of animals, a process whose beginning can be traced to the Mesolithic-Neolithic era, until the Copper and Bronze Ages. It is, however, equally certain that rearing and the planned use of animals for producing milk came about much later, since it requires a complex division of labor. Indeed, we must not forget that the starting point of such efforts began with a mammal that produced milk solely during the gestation period. Beyond these deductions, we doubt anyone can state with certainty when yogurt was discovered, if not by limiting the attribution of its origins to the distant dawn of time.

The results of studies and clues from the prehistoric era indicate with some approximation that milk was stored in sacks made of animal skin or the stomach or viscera of butchered animals. Therefore inevitably, if it was not consumed quickly and left in contact with the air, it transformed itself naturally through the action of the germs, coagulating and fermenting. Perhaps it was precisely the use of these containers and the contact with the gastric and intestinal enzymes that facilitated its acidic transformation.

Rather than an invention, yogurt can therefore be called an inevitable discovery, a causal and surprise event that created a new flavor. We like to imagine this domestic scene: A container full of milk is forgotten in the corner of a pile dwelling. Having discovered it curdled and soured, rather than throwing it out, this unknown progenitor tried to use it, thus becoming the first to discover a new flavor. This was likely not the first example, nor will it be the last of its kind in the history of humanity. Chance and time have always been the natural instigators of phenomena that have characterized and marked other phases in human evolution: alcoholic fermentation, leavening of bread, the discovery of penicillin … there are many obvious examples. People have simply cultivated and perfected them.

The fertile Asiatic crescent may have been the cradle of this new dietary technique. In fact, Europeans were introduced to cattle and dairy by the massive migrations of people from Central Asia, nomadic and warlike populations that bequeathed to us the ability to domesticate and raise cattle, and the capacity to use and transform their milk.

Continuous migrations from the Orient and the steppes of Eastern Europe favored the spread of these phenomena, which were later perfected by the warrior expeditions of Greeks, Phoenicians, Assyrian-Babylonians, Egyptians, and Romans (among whom, however, the consumption of fermented milk products was not especially widespread), which completed its diffusion in the West. On the other hand, we must wait for Columbus and the hardships that his discovery of the Americas represented for the local populations before we see the raising of livestock and the use of milk also spread through the New World.

So, in our fanciful story, we must evoke the moon and the nomadic shepherd on the steppes of Asia, two stars in the milky cosmogonies, the fermenting cosmologies, teaming with mischievous invisible enzymes, which many centuries later microbiological science would christen *lactobacillus* and *streptococcus*, depriving us of some of their magic. These "yeasts," often known as *maya* in Asiatic cultures, and which provide a fermented milk known generically in the West by the Turkish word *youghourt* (also "kefir" in the late 19th and early 20th centuries), are associated both etymologically and by custom with the concept of "long life." From the Indian dadhi, to the Egyptian benraib, to the Mongol kumis, to the Syrian leben, to the Sardinian joddu—everywhere it is known and produced—fermented milk is always associated with long-duration, prolonging life, or concepts somehow associated with physical well-being. Just as professor Ilja Metchnikoff would demonstrate a few centuries later, fermentation is in fact a positive event (think for example of fermentation tuns), and represents a defeat for the processes of degeneration. At the root of it all is milk—from goats, sheep, horses, donkeys, camels (rarely and much later, cows), and even reindeer in Northern Europe.

The secrets that have handed this food down to the current day are its elevated preservability even under special conditions (it was very common among nomadic shepherds precisely for this reason), its nutritional value and high digestibility, and its acidic flavor that makes it especially pleasant and thirst quenching.

As mentioned above, there is little traceable written history on yogurt (much better documented, although abundant only in more recent times, is the history of a later milk derivative: cheese). Rather, we find wobbly memories, rich in anecdote—something from ancient Greece, a few hints from Pliny the Elder—until nearly the Middle Ages. From the little that we do have however, we get the impression of an important food (at least initially in Eastern Europe, Asia, and the Middle East), important enough to be recorded in the two sacred books that are best known today.

The Bible (Deuteronomy) indicates that fermented milk products appeared with Moses, who considered them vital components of the diet that God gave to his people. In the Book of Genesis however, there is a hint at a mystical origin, recalling when God had the secret of yogurt brought to the patriarch Abraham. With a certain analogy, in the Islamic tradition, it is the prophet Mohammed who hands down to his people the "magic" of the transformation of milk. According to a legend well known among the shepherds who live in the mountains of the Middle East, the Prophet gave his people Kefir grains (or grains of the Prophet Mohammed) that are essential to the acidification process of milk. Many centuries later (A.D. 204 – 222) in the bibliography of the Emperor Heliogabalus, we find the recipe for *opus lactarum*, the yogurt of today with added honey and fruit.

But Eastern Europe and Asia are the true cradle of fermented milk products. The warrior women who roamed the steppes of southern Russia on horseback, the Amazons, are credited with the production of a fermented horse milk characterized by a variable alcoholic content, still known today as Kummis or Kefir.

Centuries later, a legend (which was likely inspired by the ancient methods described above) traces the spread of the consumption of fermented milk to the times of Genghis Khan: The canteen of a courier in the Mongol army was filled with milk rather than water in an attempt to place him in difficulty, trying to subject him to incredible thirst. But the plan backfired; the acidic drink (or alcoholic acid) that resulted gave the courier such renewed energy that it made an impression on Genghis Khan, who pressed the new

drink upon his people. Another leader, Francis I of France, extolled the virtues of yogurt. Suffering from intestinal troubles, he was cured by a Turkish man who, it appears, arrived at court with a flock of sheep and a mysterious recipe with which he prepared fermented milk. It is curious how the stories alternate between evidence of a thaumaturgical-curative use of yogurt and a more purely dietary use.

Even in very ancient Arabic texts there are indications of its use in the kitchen, also confirmed in the fantastical stories of the *Thousand and One Nights*. In accounts of the Crusades its consumption is reported both as part of the daily diet and in sumptuous banquets, while its use is less common in Jewish cuisine, in which it is prohibited to combine meat with milk or its derivatives in the same dish. Beyond being deemed important because their consumption makes it possible to conserve other animal proteins, in certain geographic areas (Eastern Europe, the near East) fermented milk products are also used in maturing or deodorizing when using the meat of adult or lower quality animals such as sheep or rams.

A healthy and digestible food, its regular consumption has always been associated with tangible beneficial effects on human health. These virtues were confirmed by the observations of 18th-century travelers who recorded the longevity of the Arabs in the desert, Bulgarian shepherds, and in general the populations of the Ottoman Empire, all of whom used yogurt both in their daily diets and for depurative and curative purposes.

But it was the positivist science of the early 1900s that finally revealed the secrets of this food. The first scientific studies, which eliminated the possibility for musing about fermentation by "reducing" it to a simple microbiological process, were conducted at the Pasteur Institute in Paris, and in particular by professor Ilja Metchnikoff, who was the director at the time. His theory was based on the fact that a normal diet slowly poisons the body, weakening its defenses; this occurs more rapidly if one consumes a lot of meat and limits movement. It is essential to keep the intestine free of harmful microbes; in fact, "the exclusion of damaging microbes and the introduction of beneficial microbes, such as those from the fermentation of lactic acid, must represent a great service to health." During a research trip on the steppes of Kalmuck, he attributed the longevity of the Kalmucks to their prevalent diet based on fermented milk.

In his studies on aging, he later observed that Bulgarians who lived to be over a hundred years old followed the same diet. Using a sample of yogurt from an area of Bulgaria famed for the longevity of its population, he succeeded in isolating the bacillus deemed responsible for the fermentation of milk, and from that point forward it would be called *lactobacillus bulgaricus* in their honor.

So no more "grains of Mohammed" or mischievous sprites: one of the "starters" of the milk fermentation process had been identified, which along with *streptococcus thermophilus*, acting on lactose, would transform it into lactic acid and then into the food we know as yogurt.

In 1908 professor Ilja Metchnikoff was awarded the Nobel Prize for medicine for his studies in immunology. After millennia, humankind finally had an answer, and the yogurt industry was effectively born. Professor Metchnikoff required his second wife, Olga, to prepare extravagant quantities of sour milk for his personal consumption. His collaborators and acquaintances mimicked the habit, which quickly spread through Paris, and then France. The trend soon overflowed across Europe and overseas, favoring the establishment of production factories small and large. In 1906, the company "le Ferment" in France began to sell fermented milk called *lactobacilline*; the successful spread of the product led to the introduction, in 1925, of the term "yoghourt" for the first time in the Petit Larousse dictionary as a common word. The same term was already in the first Arabic-Turkish dictionary published in Tsing-Kiang in 1701. Hundreds of thousands of years after its accidental discovery, the modern era of yogurt had begun.

ILJA METCHNIKOFF
(Nobel prize in 1908)

The Russian immunologist, observing sour milk under the microscope, discovered that the acidity was caused by a bacillus that he christened *lactobacillus bulgaricus*. From that day forward, his wife Olga had to prepare kilos of sour milk for her husband, who used it extravagantly, and yogurt spread throughout the world.

The Thousand Virtues of Yogurt

by Flavio Boraso

I f milk represents the first, and often only, food for a newborn mammal for a considerable period of its life, in adult human beings milk and the products deriving from it also play an important role, and represent a basic food that a balanced diet may exclude only with great inconvenience. It is within this framework that we should place yogurt, a product obtained using a biological type of food preservation technique (fermentation), or rather, the spontaneous or controlled acidification of the original milk. In industrial production, after correcting the fat content where necessary, the milk (generally cow's) is concentrated through evaporation and is homogenized before being heated to 195 – 200°F for 5 – 10 minutes. This rise in temperature favors both the formation of a creamy curd and also creates favorable conditions for the growth of lactic bacteria. These are then added later and will trigger the start of fermentation, which may take place directly in the final packaging or in large fermenting containers, from which it will then be removed for packaging. Yogurt is therefore a dietary product that falls into the category of fermented milk products. These, as far as nutritional value is concerned, basically reflect those of the original milk. Considering that yogurt on the market is produced largely with cow's milk, it is effectively similar to it, with the exception of modifications that can occur through intentional manipulations (as, for example, the addition of powdered milk during processing), or changes caused by the fermentation process.

In fact, the fermentation process initiates a series of transformations, the first of which is the acidification of the milk. This happens through the scission of the lactose (the sugar in milk, which is reduced by 20 – 30 percent) into two simpler components—glucose and galactose—with a consequent production of lactic acid, which moves from levels near zero in milk to 0.8 – 1.0 percent in yogurt. This transformation is caused by the milk enzymes belonging mostly to two bacterial varieties, *lactobacillus bulgaricus* and *streptococcus thermophilus* (beyond the presence of lesser quantities of various strains of *lactobacillus casei, lactobacillus acidophilus*, and *bifidobacteria*), which in quality yogurt must be alive at levels of at least 10 million microorganisms per gram of product consumed.

While the percentage of fats remains fundamentally analogous to that of the base food, the lactic fermentation also acts on the coagulation of the proteins, particularly on casein (the protein most represented in milk), improving its digestibility as compared to milk.

A primary element that emerges is therefore yogurt, which as a direct derivative of milk preserves the complexity and richness of its components while making vast improvements in digestibility thanks to the acidification process. Beyond the acidification process, it should also be remembered that milk is digested in the human body through the lactase enzyme, the availability of which decreases in step with the dietary diversification that follows weaning. This is the reason why, even with "normal" health conditions, milk is much easier to digest for a child than an adult. In humans, lactase action undergoes a gradual reduction beginning during the weaning period, until it reaches a residual level of 10 percent in adults.

This acquired lactase deficiency basically constitutes a physiological state in most of the adult population, and also coincides with intolerance and the consequent removal of milk from the diet. Under these conditions, outside lactose-free milk, yogurt occupies a privileged position in the daily diet. In fact, the transformation of lactose by the lactobacillus into two simpler elements (glucose and galactose) makes yogurt digestible even for people with a lactase deficiency.

Where protein value is concerned, values in yogurt coincide with those of milk, depending directly on the percentage representation of its fats. Precisely for this reason, recent years have witnessed a growing trend in producing reduced-fat yogurt (the so-called "light" products), which can thus become a valid alternative in low-calorie diets.

The energy content of this food is effectively rather low. The caloric intake ranges from 35 to 65 kilocalories per 100 grams of product depending on the level of lipids in the original milk. Obviously, the caloric intake increases in the case of yogurt with added sugars or fruit.

While the proportional relationships between proteins, fats, and sugars are perfectly balanced, it should be stressed how this food product also offers a modest contribution of vitamins (in particular the B group vitamins), even if their proportions also depend on the original milk, which in its turn may be influenced by the breeding conditions, the animal's diet, and by the degree of thermal treatment used in preparing the yogurt.

More significant from the dietetic point of view, however, is the contribution yogurt offers in mineral salts. The fermentation of milk does not in fact negatively influence the mineral content, of which the yogurt, like the original milk, is quite rich, especially in calcium, phosphorus, magnesium, and zinc.

Of these, the role of calcium in particular must be stressed; it remains for an extended period in our intestines in the form of calcium lactate, favoring its full absorption. This makes yogurt especially well suited for the diets of children, the elderly, and convalescents; that is, those who need calcium most. The daily requirement of calcium is greater in infancy and adolescence (up to a gram a day) than in adulthood (when it decreases to 400 – 600 milligrams), in part because of its involvement in skeletal growth and the continuous reshaping of bones. Yogurt, like milk, provides an important contribution, especially of this mineral, which plays a very important role in numerous vital functions (beyond ossification, the contraction of muscular fiber, just as in the process of blood coagulation). In cow's milk, the calcium content is an average of 120 mg per 100 g of product, and in yogurt increases from 120 to 140 mg, depending on whether the milk is whole or skim. It should not be forgotten that among all milk products, the absolute highest contribution of calcium to our bodies is supplied by cheeses. Calcium is particularly well represented in aged cheeses, such as Grana Padano, which reaches 1,300 mg per 100 g of product.

Precisely because of all of these considerations, yogurt occupies an important role in the dietary chain and is practically the only food that can replace milk in guaranteeing the daily intake of essential nutrients.

Further, its digestibility, together with the special combination of its components, makes yogurt an indispensable food for the good functioning of the digestive system. The presence of live milk enzymes and its essentially acid base (along with the presence of the B vitamin complex), allow yogurt to perform vital regulatory action in the intestine, successfully battling putrefactive and abnormal fermentative processes thanks to the stimulus it provides to the growth of intestinal flora.

Beyond these nutritional motivations, yogurt (and fermented milk products) is still widely represented in the diets of Middle Eastern and Central European countries especially, partially for historic and cultural reasons. In Italy, the consumption of yogurt is still relatively limited (6.5 kilos [14 lbs] per year per capita, compared with 15 kilos [33 lbs] in Holland and 13 kilos [29 lbs] in Switzerland). But Italian consumers are demonstrating increasing interest (especially women), and appreciate it as a quick, low-calorie snack, or as a substitute for milk (for example at breakfast with cereals or in preparing desserts).

Beyond the widespread acceptance of its flavor in a strict sense, it should also be noted that fermented milk products must also be considered beyond the mere judgment of their nutritional value, broadening this concept in line with a more modern vision of the relationships between diet, nutrition, and health. From this point of view the value of fermented milk products grows even further thanks to their probiotic nature—that is, they contain live microorganisms capable of offering a health benefit. The most common microorganisms in commercial fermented milk products, beyond the classic *lactobacillus bulgaricus* and *streptococcus thermophilus*, are the various strains of *lactobacillus casei, lactobacillus acidophilus*, and *bifidobacteria*, all of which are bacilli that are resistant to gastric and bile acids, and therefore during the digestive process can surpass the stomach to reach the intestine, where, by adhering to the intestinal wall, they provide a rather effective barrier against possible pathogenic agents, among other benefits. The properties we understand today about probiotic foods are likely those same health virtues that have made fermented milk products famous through the centuries.

Alternating between myth and legend since prehistoric times, it was not until the early 1900s that the Russian scholar Ilja Metchnikoff first explained in scientific terms his observations on the abilities of fermented milk products to positively influence human health and aging. His observations, first published in French (*Essai Optimistic*), were soon translated into a better-known English version (*The prolongation of life: optimistic studies*) and quickly spread around the world.

But Professor Metchnikoff himself called for caution against simplistic fervor, and put faith in the fact that "future studies may clarify the role of fermented milk products in contributing to delaying and improving aging." Despite these cautions, he was accused of naïveté, or improper use of science and errors in judgment.

Thus, fermented milk products did not have an entirely positive effect on the scientist's life. Basically, only the rigor and method of studies in the last 30 years have helped clarify the most reliable information on what may be considered the "virtues" of fermented milk products. In part, this is because the miraculous expectations tied to the use of fermented milk products were perpetuated through the years but were based on anecdotal evidence or poorly controlled studies. Only recently have the concepts of Metchnikoff been joined by those of probiosis—that is, the beneficial effects supplied by live bacterial cultures ingested in quantities sufficient to surpass the gastric barrier and reach the intestinal tract. On the basis of this evidence, today it is more credible to state that, beyond the better-known and predictable effect on lactose, which is rendered more digestible by the action of the bacteria, there are other medical applications for yogurt related to the action of the milk enzymes. Yogurt can in fact to be used for its antidiarrhoeal action in fighting dysentery caused by bacteria or dietary imbalances; to regenerate intestinal bacterial flora during or after antibiotic therapy; in alleviating chronic constipation; and as a substitute for milk in the case of digestive problems or allergies.

There are still other probiotic effects that are soliciting a great deal of interest among researchers, as for example, among those related to the ingestion of this food: a stimulus to the immune system (representing the body's defenses against disease), a reduction in blood cholesterol values with consequent control of events related to arteriosclerosis, and the prevention of intestinal forms of tumors thanks to the opposition it offers against agents that favor tumoral development.

Here is the point of contact between science, which illuminates, and legend, which hands down the virtues of this food across the millennia. Here is the importance of this food, understood in the strict dietary sense, but even more in a health-related sense. A history of accidental events, of the mysterious encounter between humanity and the microscopic world that surrounds it, and all that transforms being and becoming: the mystery of life and the rules that shape it.

Yogurt under the Law

by Chiara Busso

On the basis of an analysis prepared by the Italian Health Ministry, fermented milk products are "products obtained through the coagulation of milk without the removal of whey, through the exclusive action of the microorganisms of prevalently acidic, or acidic-alcoholic, fermentation, specific in each ferment, kept alive and vital in elevated quantities." These products are prepared using full cream, semi-skimmed, or skim milk, making sure it is free of antibiotics and is derived from dairy cows certified free of mastitis. The milk must be homogenized and then pasteurized at 195 – 200°F for 5 – 20 seconds to destroy any microorganisms present, followed by the concentration process (up to 14 percent solids), which serves to improve product consistency. Alternatively, cream may be added. At this point a culture of lactic bacteria—more commonly called enzymes—is injected, known as "starter." The microorganisms ferment a portion of their lactose, transforming it into lactic acid (that is, yogurt), or else into lactic acid and ethyl alcohol (that is, kefir).

As far as packaging is concerned, preservation must occur at a temperature of no greater than 39°F for one month; if the product was heat-stabilized it may be stored at higher temperatures for up to three months.

The market today also offers fermented milk products with various additions (in a maximum proportion of 30 percent compared with the milk) of fruit (in all its forms), natural essences, distilled flavors, cocoa, chocolate, honey, and many more. Milk-based desserts are very similar to yogurt, but only in appearance. They have a low level of acidity and a creamy texture, and contain no live and vital lactic bacteria. These products may be sold with the name "yogurt" only in Holland and Great Britain.

	WHOLE YOGURT	LOW FAT YOGURT
DRY MATTER	5.2 – 12.0	9.7 – 12.7
PROTEINS	3.6 – 5.0	3.3 – 5.0
FAT	3.0 – 3.5	0.5 – 0.9
SUGAR (LACTOSE)	4.8 – 5.3	5.1 – 5.6
LACTIC ACID	0.9 – 1.3	1.0 – 1.6
PH	3.6 – 4.1	3.6 – 4.1

The table on page 27 shows that the nutritional value of whole yogurt is greater than skim, which, however, is much better indicated for low-calorie diets.

The use of powdered milk, or even milk intended for animal consumption, is one of the most frequent types of fraud. The law, however, permits the use of milk from non-bovine species, as long as the correct denomination is displayed on the packaging, as for example "goat's milk" or "sheep's milk" yogurt.

From a nutritional and therapeutic point of view fermented milk products offer many advantages.

In fact, yogurt:

- Regenerates intestinal flora, especially after the use of antibiotics.

- Destroys pathogenic germs, ensuring a balance of bacterial flora and, because it fights harmful bacteria, is particularly useful in the case of dietary imbalances or colitis.

- Releases the enzymes that aid digestion and intestinal assimilation of lactose and fatty proteins.

- Supports the metabolism of bile acids during digestion.

- Synthesizes B6 group vitamins through the bacteria it contains (compared to milk, yogurt contains less vitamin B12, but more vitamin B6).

- Contains various substances (principally lactic acid and other organic acids) that protect the digestive system. According to recent studies, yogurt produces a minimal quantity of peroxide that inhibits certain microbes, acting as a buffer; that is, it resists strong acidification or alkalinization and detoxifies.

- Lubricates the intestine through a supply of homogenized fats and water.

Yogurt in the Kitchen

by Enza Bettelli

Anyone who loves yogurt appreciates the velvety consistency that melts gently between tongue and palate. Acidity is the other element that gives yogurt its special flavor, though not everyone appreciates this characteristic, and there are some who forgo this healthy and beneficial food in favor of others with a perhaps more delicate flavor that may not be of equal dietary importance. This acidity is obviously more prominent in white yogurt, especially of the low fat variety, but this can be easily mitigated by mixing in a pinch of table salt, which dissolves evenly. If you're not especially worried about calorie counting, you can also add a spoonful or two of honey, mixing carefully until it is fully incorporated. Another method for tempering the acidity of yogurt is to combine it with fruit, sweet or starchy vegetables (e.g., potatoes, peas, carrots), cereal flakes, or bread.

Yogurt gives the best of itself when eaten on an empty stomach, at breakfast or as a snack, and in many cases gives relief when the stomach or digestive system are bilious. A cup of yogurt is also useful before bedtime in fighting insomnia, after an abundant intake of alcohol to rebalance the body, or spread on the skin in the case of dermatitis or sunburns to help relieve burning and itching.

In the kitchen, yogurt is an equally valuable and versatile ingredient. It helps enliven the slightly flat flavor of some dishes, and is equally useful in toning down a hot or salty sting in others. That's quite impressive, when you think that often just a spoonful of yogurt is enough to achieve the desired effect. It is also an excellent substitute for cream in many recipes and for oil as a condiment for salads. When mixed with certain cold sauces (e.g., mayonnaise, tartare, etc.), it provides volume while adding very few fats.

The merits of yogurt are tied in good part to the presence of live bacteria that survive at low temperatures but not at high temperatures. It is therefore vital to avoid prolonged cooking over a high flame or in a very hot oven. The ideal method would be to add the yogurt to the recipe after it has been removed from the heat, or at least near the end of the cooking period. To improve its performance, it is advisable to use it at room temperature, blending with a bit of starch dissolved in a spoonful of water before adding it to the cooking base or sauces, which will prevent it from forming lumps. When used in desserts, the addition of a pinch of baking soda helps achieve a perfect rise. Cooking on the burner should be done quickly, without covering the pot, to prevent the condensation from falling back into the pot and dividing the solid part of the yogurt from the whey. Always stir in the same direction to blend everything more easily.

HOMEMADE YOGURT

The basics required to make yogurt at home are live enzymes that should be purchased every two weeks at the pharmacy or dairy plant. For intervening mixtures, a pot of the freshly made yogurt may be set aside and used as a base. When using a yogurt maker simply follow the instructions, using milk (possibly UHT milk), heated to 107 – 113°F, into which will be mixed the live enzymes or yogurt before dividing the mixture into the pots of the yogurt maker. For a thicker or denser yogurt, add a spoonful of powdered skim milk.

When making yogurt without a yogurt maker, the hot milk mixed with the enzymes or the retained yogurt (and possibly with powdered milk) should be poured into a wide-neck thermos, also heated, and then sealed tightly and left to sit for approximately 12 hours. Then check the consistency of the mixture. Finally, pour the yogurt into containers and store in the refrigerator.

aperitifs

Emotion in Blue

Serves 6
- 2 parts apple juice • 1 part vodka • ice cubes
- 1 splash Blue Curaçao • 1 part yogurt, drained
- Optional garnishes: apple slices, strawberries, and mint sprigs

Combine the apple juice, vodka, ice, and Blue Curaçao in a shaker and shake. Spoon the yogurt into the bottom of each cocktail glass and gently strain the cocktail on top. Garnish with the fruit and mint.

White Caribbean

Serves 6
- 2 parts pineapple juice • 1 part coconut milk • 1 splash lime juice
- ice cubes • shaved ice • 1 part yogurt, drained
- Optional garnish: slices of exotic fruit

Shake together the pineapple juice, coconut milk, lime juice, and ice cubes. Place shaved ice and yogurt in the bottom of each glass. Top with the cocktail and garnish with your favorite exotic fruit.

Merida

Serves 6
- 1 part tequila • 1 part gin • 1 splash lime juice
- ice cubes • 1 part yogurt, drained
- Optional garnishes: slices of lime and red currants

Shake together the tequila, gin, and lime juice with ice. Place yogurt in the bottom of each glass, then strain the cocktail on top. Garnish with the fresh fruit.

appetizers

Tuna Carpaccio
on Yogurt and Green Onion Cream with Apple Cider Vinegar

Serves 6
- ½ cup yogurt, drained • 3.5 oz. mascarpone cheese • salt
- freshly ground white pepper • 1 bunch chives, finely chopped
- extra virgin olive oil • 4 small green onions, thinly sliced
- 3 tbsp. apple cider vinegar • 1 14-oz. tuna fillet, very thinly sliced

In a bowl, gently whisk the yogurt and mascarpone cheese, adding the salt, white pepper, chives, and a healthy spoonful of olive oil. In another bowl, mix the green onions with the apple cider vinegar, a pinch of salt, and a drizzle of olive oil. Place a spoonful of the yogurt-mascarpone mixture on each plate or in each champagne glass. Top with the tuna slices. Garnish with the marinated green onion and a drizzle of olive oil.

Wine
Pairings

Lamb Loin
Marinated in Yogurt with Garlic and Tarragon Infused Oil

Serves 6

For the lamb loins • 1½ cups yogurt • 2 garlic cloves, minced • ½ white onion, roughly chopped • 1 medium carrot, roughly chopped • 1 bay leaf • 1 marjoram sprig • 1 rosemary sprig • 3 lamb loins • salt • freshly ground white pepper • extra virgin olive oil

For the garlic and tarragon oil • 1½ cups first press extra virgin olive oil • scant ¼ cup minced garlic • 5 – 6 fresh tarragon sprigs

Preparing the lamb loins In a bowl, combine the yogurt, garlic, onion, carrot, and herbs. Add the lamb loins and cover with plastic wrap, allowing the meat to marinate in the refrigerator for at least 3 hours. Dry the lamb loins and season generously on both sides with salt and pepper to taste. In a nonstick pan, heat a drizzle of oil and cook the lamb until medium rare.

Preparing the garlic and tarragon oil In a blender, puree the oil, garlic, and tarragon and allow to sit for at least 3 hours. Strain.

Plating Slice the loins while they are still warm and divide among the dinner plates. Drizzle with the garlic-tarragon oil.

Wine Pairings

Salmon and Yogurt Mousse
Quenelles with Papaya Sauce
Perfumed with Pink Pepper

Serves 6

For the salmon mousse • 2 tsp. powdered gelatin (less than 1 envelope)
• 1⅓ lbs. extremely fresh salmon fillets, skin and bones removed
• ⅓ cup yogurt, drained • ½ cup heavy cream, whipped to soft peaks
• salt • freshly ground white pepper • extra virgin olive oil

For the papaya sauce • extra virgin olive oil • 1 small white onion, chopped
• 2 very ripe papayas, peeled, pitted, and diced • salt • freshly ground white pepper
• 1 oz. pickled pink pepper grains

For optional garnish • papaya slices • freshly ground pink pepper

Preparing the quenelles In a bowl that will fit comfortably over a pan of simmering water, sprinkle the gelatin over a small amount of cold water and leave, without stirring, until it swells and becomes spongy, about 3 – 5 minutes. Then place the bowl over the pan of simmering water, stirring, until clear. Set aside. Puree the salmon fillets in a blender, slowly adding the yogurt and gelatin. Then add the cream, salt, pepper, and a drizzle of olive oil to achieve a smooth and creamy consistency. Pour the mixture into a container and leave it in the refrigerator for about two hours.

Preparing the papaya sauce Preheat a sauté pan with the oil and sauté the onion over low heat. Add the diced papaya, salt, and white pepper, cooking over low heat for about 5 minutes. Allow the mixture to cool, then process in a blender and strain. Add the pink pepper and allow to sit for at least 40 minutes.

Plating Remove mousse from the fridge and, with a large spoon, form quenelles. Spoon papaya sauce on each plate and top with quenelles. Garnish with papaya and pink pepper.

Wine
Pairings

Spring Vegetable Pearls
in Yogurt and Black Olive Sauce
with Watercress Olive Oil

Serves 6

For the vegetable pearls • 2 zucchini, peeled • 3 carrots, peeled • 2 beets, peeled • 1 celeriac (celery root), peeled • 3 white radishes • 4 new potatoes, peeled

For the yogurt sauce • 1 scant cup yogurt, drained • 5 oz. meaty black olives, pitted and finely chopped • extra virgin olive oil • salt • cayenne pepper • 1 tbsp. mascarpone cheese

For the watercress oil • 3½ oz. watercress, divided into thirds • 5¼ oz. extra virgin olive oil • freshly ground black pepper

For optional garnish • 5 oz. meaty black olives • watercress leaves

Preparing the vegetable pearls With a melon baller, carve the vegetables into small pearls and cook them separately in lots of salted boiling water. Then transfer them to a bowl of ice water. After about 30 seconds, drain and place them on a cotton cloth to dry.

Preparing the yogurt sauce Mix the yogurt with the olives, olive oil, salt, and cayenne pepper. Then add the mascarpone cheese and continue mixing until it is completely incorporated.

Preparing the watercress oil In the blender, mince one third of the watercress, remove from the blender, and set aside. Blend some olive oil with the pepper and remaining watercress. Allow to sit for an hour, then filter with a very fine strainer. Finish by stirring in the minced watercress and additional olive oil if necessary.

Plating Place the pearls in the center of each plate. Coat one section with the yogurt sauce, and carefully drizzle watercress oil around the inside edge of the plate. Garnish with a few olives and watercress leaves.

Wine
Pairings

Shredded Smoked Beef Jerky

with Capers and Wild Herb Yogurt

Serves 6
- scant ½ cup yogurt, drained
- 2 heaping tbsp. high-quality capers, drained
- 1 small bunch wild herb leaves (watercress, chives, dill, parsley)
- salt • extra virgin olive oil • 18 oz. shredded beef jerky

For optional garnish • herb sprigs

In the blender, puree the yogurt, capers, and the wild herbs with some salt and a drizzle of olive oil. Arrange the jerky in the middle of each plate, surround it with the yogurt sauce, and garnish with a few herb sprigs.

Wine
Pairings

Soups

Oxtail Consommé

with Watercress Cherry Tomatoes and Dumplings with Yogurt

Serves 6

For the consommé • 5 quarts beef consommé • 1 oxtail, about 4½ lbs.
• 1 carrot, peeled • 1 yellow onion, peeled • salt

For the watercress tomatoes • 12 cherry tomatoes, quartered
• 1½ cups watercress, lightly chopped

For the dumplings • 5 oz. lean veal • ¼ cup yogurt, drained • 2 egg whites
• salt • freshly ground white pepper

Preparing the oxtail consommé In a stockpot or large saucepot, combine the beef consommé with the oxtail, carrot, and onion, and simmer over very low heat for 3½ hours. Strain and season with salt, discarding the oxtail and vegetables.

Preparing the watercress tomatoes Place the cherry tomatoes and watercress in a bowl and let sit for an hour.

Preparing the dumplings Pulse the meat in a food processor until a smooth paste forms. Pulse again, slowly adding the yogurt, egg whites, salt, and pepper. Shape six dumplings and cook in a small portion of the consommé for about 2 minutes or until cooked through.

Plating Divide the consommé among six soup bowls and serve with a few dumplings and some watercress tomatoes.

Wine
Pairings

Potato Soup
with Diced Truffles in Yogurt
with a Bread Crust

Serves 6

For the soup • extra virgin olive oil • 2 white onions, peeled and minced • 2 lbs. potatoes, peeled and diced • 2 bay leaves • 1 stalk celery, halved • 1 carrot, peeled and halved • ½ cup dry white wine • 2 quarts beef stock • salt • freshly ground white pepper

For the yogurt • 1 black truffle, diced • ¼ cup yogurt, drained

For the crust • 10 oz. bread dough • 1 egg yolk • 6 tbsp. grated cheese, such as Fontina • 3 tbsp. butter, sliced

Preparing the soup Heat a drizzle of oil in a medium-large saucepot and cook the onion over low heat until golden. Add the potatoes, bay leaves, celery, and carrot. Sauté, carefully add the white wine, and bring to a boil. When the wine is completely evaporated, add the beef broth and bring to a boil. Cook over moderate heat until the potatoes are nearly cooked. Remove the bay leaves, carrot, and celery and season with salt and white pepper.

Preparing the yogurt Place the truffle in the yogurt to marinate. Set aside.

Preparing the crust and plating Pour the soup into small, deep oven-safe bowls, distributing the truffle yogurt evenly among them. Divide the bread dough into six balls of equal size, roll them out with a rolling pin, and cover each bowl of soup completely with the dough. Brush the dough with the egg yolk, sprinkle with the grated cheese, and place a piece of butter in the middle. Bake at 475°F until the crust is golden; serve.

Wine Pairings

Purée of Curried Shrimp
Soup with Yogurt

Serves 6
- 1 lb. fresh shrimp, peeled, shells reserved
- extra virgin olive oil • 1 medium white onion, peeled and diced
- 1 medium carrot, peeled and diced • 1 bay leaf • ⅔ cup flour
- ½ cup brandy • curry powder to taste • salt • ½ cup yogurt, drained

Place the shrimp in ice water. Heat olive oil in a stockpot or large saucepot. Add the onion and carrot and brown. Then add the shrimp shells and bay leaf. Sauté for 5 minutes over low-medium heat. Sprinkle the mixture with flour and mix thoroughly with a wooden spoon. Remove from heat. Carefully and gradually pour in the brandy and stir well. Place back on the heat and flambé. Meanwhile, in another large pot, cook the shrimp in at least 3 quarts of salted boiling water. Set aside the shrimp and cooking water. Pour 2½ quarts of this shrimp cooking water over the vegetable and shrimp shell mixture, bring to a boil, and simmer for about 35 minutes. When the soup reaches a velvety consistency, pass it through a strainer into another pot. Add the curry to taste, mixing gently with a whisk. Return to a boil and add the cooked shrimp. Season with salt and serve with drizzles of yogurt and olive oil.

Wine
Pairings

Iced Tomato Soup
with Basil Yogurt

Serves 6
- 2 lbs. very ripe tomatoes, peeled, seeds removed, and cubed
- 1 quart condensed meat broth, cold, divided in thirds
- salt • freshly ground black pepper • extra virgin olive oil
- 1 small bunch basil leaves, minced • ⅔ cup yogurt, drained

In a blender, puree the tomatoes with two thirds of the condensed meat broth. Add the salt, black pepper, and olive oil. Place in the freezer for about 20 minutes until the soup is nearly frozen. Meanwhile, mix the basil leaves into the yogurt and add a pinch of salt and black pepper. Set aside. Remove the semi-frozen soup from the freezer and stir in the remaining cold condensed meat broth. Ladle into soup bowls, placing a spoonful of basil yogurt in the center of each soup bowl. Complete with a drizzle of olive oil.

Wine
Pairings

first courses

Dumplings with Asparagus

and Yogurt over Tomato Purée

Serves 6

For the tomato purée • extra virgin olive oil • ½ white onion, minced
• 10 oz. tomato slices • 1 knob butter • salt • extra virgin olive oil

For the pasta • 7 oz. white asparagus, boiled • 7 oz. green asparagus, boiled
• 1⅓ cups Parmiggiano-Reggiano cheese • ¼ cup yogurt, drained
• 2 egg yolks, plus additional for forming dumplings • ½ cup breadcrumbs
• 2½ oz. ricotta cheese • salt • 18 oz. fresh egg pasta

Preparing the tomato purée In a skillet, heat the oil. Sauté the onion, add the tomato slices, and cook over very low heat for 5 minutes. Process the tomato and onion mixture in a blender with a pat of butter, salt, and a splash of oil.

Preparing the dumplings Cut the asparagus stems into ¼-inch cubes, reserving the whole tips for garnish. In a medium bowl, combine the asparagus cubes with the Parmiggiano-Reggiano cheese, yogurt, egg yolks, breadcrumbs, ricotta, and salt. Roll out the pasta dough and cut it into 2½-inch squares. Place a teaspoon of filling in the middle of each square, brush the edges with egg yolk, and fold in a triangle. Cook in salted water, drain, and serve with the tomato purée.

Wine
Pairings

Black Lasagna
with Cuttlefish and Yogurt Ragù and Green Bean Sauce

Serves 6

For the green bean sauce • 18 oz. green beans • extra virgin olive oil • ½ cup fresh cream • salt • freshly ground black pepper

For the lasagna • extra virgin olive oil • 1 white onion, chopped into small cubes • 1 garlic clove, minced • 1 bay leaf • 18 oz. cleaned cuttlefish, cut into thin strips • flour for sprinkling • ½ cup dry white wine • 1 quart fish broth • salt • freshly ground black pepper • scant ½ cup yogurt, drained • 12 sheets black lasagna

For the optional garnish • 6 sprigs parsley

Preparing the green bean sauce Boil the green beans in salted water, and cool them in ice water. Drain. Coarsely chop and blend in a food processor with a splash of olive oil, the cream, and salt and pepper until liquid.

Preparing the lasagna filling In a very large skillet, heat the oil and add the onion, garlic, and bay leaf. Brown the garlic and onion over medium heat. Add the cuttlefish and sauté for approximately 3 minutes. Sprinkle with flour and stir well. Gradually add the wine and fish broth and bring to a boil. Simmer over medium-low heat until the cuttlefish is cooked and the sauce is smooth, stirring well. Remove the bay leaf, add salt and pepper, and slowly stir in the yogurt. Cook the lasagna in salted water. Drain. To serve, place the first sheet on each plate and cover with the filling mixture. Then repeat with a second sheet of lasagna and more filling mixture. Spoon the green bean sauce alongside. Garnish each plate with a sprig of parsley.

Wine
Pairings

Pappardelle
in a Spring Sauce with Yogurt

Serves 6
- extra virgin olive oil • 10 zucchini flowers, julienned
- 1 small zucchini, julienned • 1 small carrot, peeled and julienned
- 1 small leek, julienned • 1 red pepper, julienned • ¼ cup cornstarch
- 1 pint vegetable broth • ½ avocado, pureed in a blender • cayenne pepper
- salt • 18 oz. pappardelle pasta • scant ½ cup yogurt, drained

In a preheated pan, add a drizzle of olive oil, the zucchini flowers, zucchini, carrot, leek, and pepper, and sauté over low-medium heat until crisp-tender, about 3 – 5 minutes. Over medium heat, sprinkle with the cornstarch, stir well, and gradually pour in the vegetable broth, stirring constantly. Bring to a simmer and cook, stirring, until smooth. Stir in the pureed avocado, cayenne, salt, and a drizzle of olive oil. Simmer, stirring, until well incorporated. Cook the pasta in salted boiling water, drain, and add to the spring sauce. Stir in the yogurt and serve.

Wine
Pairings

Smoked Sturgeon Risotto

with Yogurt and Prosecco

Serves 6
- extra virgin olive oil • 2 shallots, minced
- 4 oz. smoked sturgeon, cubed • 1 cup Prosecco, divided in half
- 2⅓ cups Arborio rice • About 9 cups fish broth • salt
- freshly ground black pepper • scant ½ cup yogurt, drained
- lemon slices • mint leaves

In a large skillet, heat oil and sauté the shallot over medium heat until soft, about 3 minutes. Then add the sturgeon and half of the Prosecco; boil until the wine is mostly reduced. Add the rice and sauté for about 1 minute. Over medium-high heat, add the broth in 1-cup portions, simmering and repeating until the rice is cooked, about 18 – 20 minutes. Season with salt and pepper. In a bowl, mix the yogurt with the remaining Prosecco and season with salt. Serve the risotto on dinner plates, placing a spoonful of Prosecco yogurt on the side. Garnish with lemon slices and mint leaves.

Wine Pairings

Tagliolini
in a Forest Mushroom Sauce with Thyme and Yogurt

Serves 6
- extra virgin olive oil • ½ white onion, chopped
- 1 garlic clove, minced • a few fresh thyme leaves
- 7 oz. assorted fresh mushrooms (porcini, chanterelle, cremini, shiitake), very thinly sliced • 2 tbsp. cornstarch • ½ cup white wine
- ½ cup vegetable broth • salt • freshly ground black pepper
- 18 oz. fresh tagliolini pasta (paglia e fieno), cooked and drained
- ¼ cup yogurt, drained

Slowly heat olive oil in a skillet. Over medium-high heat, brown the onion and garlic with a few thyme leaves. Add the mushroom slices and continue to sauté for another few minutes. Sprinkle with cornstarch and mix well. Gradually add the white wine and bring to a boil, stirring. Once the wine has evaporated, add the vegetable broth and bring to a simmer. Season with salt and black pepper, add the cooked pasta, and toss with the yogurt and a drizzle of olive oil, without returning to the heat. Serve.

Wine Pairings

Braised Penne
with Caviar and Yogurt
in a Vodka Sauce

Serves 6
- extra virgin olive oil • 17 oz. half penne pasta • 2 shallots, chopped
- ½ cup vodka • 3 tbsp. cornstarch • salt • freshly ground black pepper
- 1 bunch chives, finely chopped, plus some whole strands for garnish
- ¼ cup yogurt, drained • 2 oz. caviar or lumpfish roe

Preheat a nonstick pan and add a drizzle of oil. Pour in the pasta and braise until they turn a golden brown color. Set aside. In another pan, heat a drizzle of olive oil and sauté the shallots. Off the heat, carefully add the vodka. Place back on the heat, stir in the cornstarch, mix well, and bring to a simmer. Sprinkle with a bit of salt and pepper, and finish with the chives. In a bowl, combine the yogurt, caviar, and some oil. Boil the browned pasta in salted water, drain, and toss with the yogurt mixture. Add part of the vodka sauce and arrange on the plates. Garnish the plates with the remaining vodka sauce and strands of chive.

Wine
Pairings

second courses

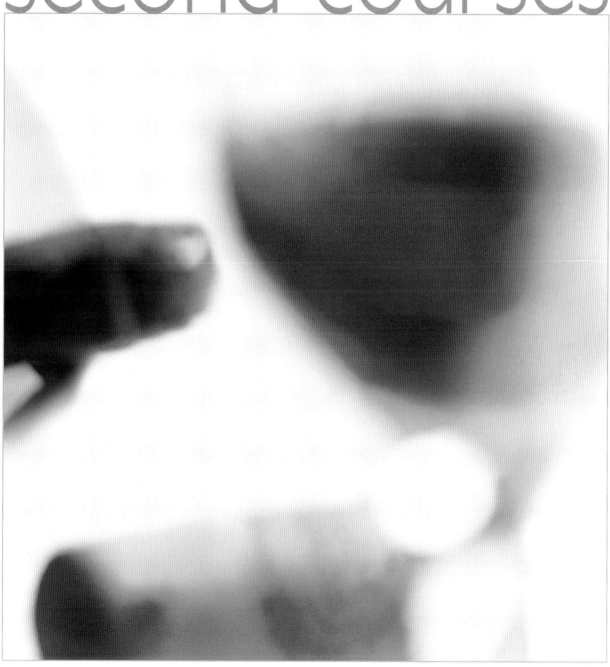

Lamb Fricassee
with Yogurt and Lemon Zest

Serves 9
- 4½ lbs. lamb leg meat, cut into ½-inch pieces • salt • freshly ground white pepper
- flour for sprinkling • extra virgin olive oil • 1 white onion, finely chopped
- ½ cup dry white wine • 1 bay leaf • about 3 quarts lamb or chicken broth
- freshly grated zest of 1 lemon • ⅓ cup yogurt

Sprinkle the lamb with salt, pepper, and flour. Heat a large skillet with oil and brown the meat over high heat. Transfer to a platter. Add the onion and sauté until golden, then carefully pour in the white wine and bring to a boil. Once the wine has evaporated completely, return the lamb to the pan with the bay leaf. Add half of the stock, bring to a boil, reduce to a simmer, and cook covered over low-medium heat until cooked through. Check the pot halfway through; you will probably need to add the other half of the broth. Halfway through cooking, also add the salt and pepper. Stir the lemon zest into the yogurt and add the mixture to the dish just before serving, removing the pan from the burner.

Wine
Pairings

Leg of Rabbit
Stuffed with Porcini Mushrooms and Yogurt in a Rosé Wine Sauce

Serves 6

For the stuffing • 10 oz. fresh porcini mushrooms • 2 egg whites
• ½ cup grated Parmiggiano-Reggiano cheese • 1 bunch parsley, leaves minced
• ¼ cup yogurt, drained • salt • freshly ground white pepper • extra virgin olive oil
• 1 white onion, finely chopped • 5 medium slices stale bread, cut into ¼-inch cubes

For the rabbit • 6 legs of rabbit, de-boned • flour • 2 shallots, minced
• 3 cups rosé wine, divided in half • 2 quarts light rabbit stock, divided in half
• ⅓ cup potato starch, if necessary

Preparing the stuffing Blend the porcini mushrooms, egg whites, Parmiggiano-Reggiano cheese, parsley, and yogurt in a food processor, adjusting with salt and pepper to taste. In a skillet, heat the oil and brown the onion. Then add the bread cubes and continue to brown for another 2 – 3 minutes. Combine the mushroom mixture with the warm bread in a bowl and stir with a wooden spoon.

Preparing the rabbit Stuff the rabbit legs with the mushroom/bread mixture, and secure with toothpicks or sew shut with kitchen twine. In a Dutch oven, heat a drizzle of oil, sprinkle the stuffed legs with salt, pepper, and a pinch of flour, and brown them completely on all sides. When the legs are browned, remove them from the pan. Add the shallots and sauté over medium heat until soft. Add half of the wine and boil until almost evaporated. Return the rabbit legs to the pot and cover with the remaining wine and half of the light rabbit stock. Bring to a boil, reduce heat, cover, and simmer over low-medium heat for approximately 30 minutes, until cooked through. If necessary, thicken the sauce with potato starch. Before serving, remove the legs from the pot and place them on a platter. Then strain the sauce through a sieve. Slice the legs and arrange each one in a fan on each dinner plate, coating with the sauce.

Wine
Pairings

Ostrich

Marinated in Yogurt with Vegetables, Braised in Sagrantino di Montefalco Wine

Serves 6
- 2¼ lbs. cubed ostrich meat • 1 scant cup yogurt
- extra virgin olive oil • 1 red onion, cut into small cubes
- salt • freshly ground black pepper • flour for sprinkling
- 1.5 quarts Sagrantino di Montefalco wine • 1 quart beef or ostrich stock
- 10 oz. carrots, peeled and cut into oblong shapes
- 7 oz. potatoes, peeled and cut into oblong shapes

Marinate the ostrich meat in the yogurt for at least 2 hours. Heat the oil in a Dutch oven and sauté the onion until brown. Drain the ostrich meat from the yogurt, sprinkle the meat with salt, pepper, and flour and add to the pan. Brown the ostrich thoroughly and add 2 cups of the wine. Bring the wine to a boil. Once the liquid has evaporated, add the remaining wine and stock. Bring to a boil, reduce heat, cover, and simmer the meat for about 20 minutes. Then add the carrots and the potatoes and continue braising over low heat until the meat is fully cooked. Serve.

Wine
Pairings

Strips of Chicken
Seasoned with Yogurt, Garlic, and Paprika Zabaglione

Serves 6

For the chicken • 6 chicken breast halves, skin removed and cut into thin strips
• salt • freshly ground white pepper • potato starch for sprinkling
• 1 drizzle extra virgin olive oil • 2 garlic cloves • ½ cup dry white wine
• ½ cup chicken or vegetable broth • scant ½ cup yogurt, drained
For the paprika zabaglione • 2 egg yolks • fresh juice of ½ lemon, strained
• 1 tbsp. apple cider vinegar • cayenne pepper • sweet paprika
• drizzle extra virgin olive oil • salt

Preparing the chicken Sprinkle the chicken strips with salt, pepper, and potato starch. In a relatively large pan, heat a drizzle of olive oil and sauté the garlic. Once it is golden, remove it from the pan and discard. Arrange the chicken strips in the hot oil and fry gently and carefully. Then add the white wine, a little bit at a time. Next, add the broth and bring to a boil over a low flame for another 2 – 3 minutes. Add salt and pepper, and remove from heat. Before serving, gently stir in the yogurt.

Preparing the zabaglione Bring a saucepan with a few inches of water to a simmer. Combine the egg yolks, lemon juice, apple cider vinegar, a pinch of cayenne pepper, and sweet paprika to taste in a bowl that will sit comfortably on top of the saucepan. Place the bowl on top of the pan and whisk the mixture gently (do not allow the bowl to touch the water). Add the olive oil in a slow stream while continuing to whisk until thick. Adjust seasoning with additional paprika and salt if necessary. Remove the bowl from the hot water and set aside.

Plating Serve the chicken strips on dinner plates, with the paprika zabaglione on the side.

Wine
Pairings

Veal Roulade
with Yogurt, Bacon, and Almonds

Serves 6
- 12 slices milk-fed veal loin • 1 scant cup yogurt, divided in half (one half drained)
- ⅓ cup plus 1 tbsp. peeled and chopped almonds • ½ cup Pecorino cheese shavings
- 2 tbsp. extra virgin olive oil • 1 clove garlic, minced • salt
- freshly ground black pepper • 12 medium slices bacon

Marinate the veal slices with the undrained half of the yogurt in a bowl for at least 1 hour. Combine remaining (drained) yogurt, almonds, cheese, olive oil, garlic, salt, and pepper in a bowl and mix well. Retrieve the veal slices, dry them with paper towels, and arrange a slice of bacon on each slice. Divide the stuffing into 12 portions, placing one dollop on each strip of bacon. Roll each slice closed and secure with toothpicks. In a nonstick pan, heat a bit of extra virgin olive oil, and brown each roulade thoroughly on all sides. Serve with fresh vegetables of your choice.

Wine
Pairings

Steamed Monkfish Tail

*with Yogurt Mousse
and Shavings of Candied Citron*

Serves 6
- 3 egg yolks • salt • cayenne pepper • 1 tbsp. balsamic vinegar
- ⅓ cup yogurt, drained • 5 drops fresh lemon juice, strained
- 12 monkfish tail medallions • extra virgin olive oil
- 2 oz. candied citron

Bring water to a simmer in a saucepot. Combine the egg yolks, salt, and cayenne pepper in a bowl that fits comfortably over the saucepot. Whisk, and slowly blend in the balsamic vinegar, yogurt, and drops of lemon juice. Place the bowl over the pan of simmering water and beat until you have a light foam. Steam the monkfish and then serve on dinner plates, partially coating with the yogurt mousse. Finish with a drizzle of olive oil and candied citron.

Wine
Pairings

Stacked Gilthead Fillets
with Yogurt, Zucchini, and Sauvignon Sauce

Serves 6

For the fish • About 2 lbs. gilthead or other sea bream fillets, skinned and boned • 2 cups yogurt, drained • salt
• freshly ground white pepper • fresh tarragon, finely chopped
• 3 small zucchini with dense flesh, sliced into thin strips

For the sauce • extra virgin olive oil • 1 shallot, minced
• 2 tbsp. potato starch • ½ cup Sauvignon wine • ½ cup fish broth
• 1 sprinkle fresh lemon juice, strained

For the optional garnishes • lemon slices and tarragon sprigs

Preparing the fish Place the fish on a greased baking sheet. Brush with yogurt and sprinkle with salt, pepper, and tarragon. Arrange the zucchini one by one on the fillets. Brush again with the yogurt, sprinkle with salt, pepper, and tarragon, and bake in an oven preheated to 400°F for about 10 minutes.

Preparing the sauce In a small skillet, heat the oil and gently sauté the shallot. Sprinkle with the starch, stir, and gradually add the wine and fish broth, stirring well. Bring to a slow boil for 5 minutes. Add salt, pepper, and a splash of lemon juice. The sauce should be slightly velvety and shiny.

Plating Cut each fillet in half crosswise. On each plate, arrange the cuts of gilthead one on top of another. Pour the Sauvignon sauce over the fish, and garnish with a slice of lemon and a sprig of tarragon.

Wine
Pairings

Sole Skewers
with Lemon, Aromatic Spring Herbs, and Yogurt

Serves 6
- 6 medium-size sole fillets, skinned and boned
- fresh juice of 2 lemons, strained and divided in half
- 1 bunch fresh herbs (thyme, marjoram, mint, chives), minced
- ¼ cup yogurt, drained • salt • extra virgin olive oil • ½ cup semolina flour

For optional garnish • herb bouquets

Place the sole in a bowl with half of the lemon juice, a pinch of the minced herbs, yogurt, salt, and a drizzle of oil. Cover with plastic wrap and place in the refrigerator for approximately 3 hours. Retrieve the sole fillets from the marinade and arrange them on parchment paper. Sprinkle each individual fillet with additional minced herbs and salt and roll, piercing with toothpicks or short skewers to secure. Heat a pan with some olive oil, sprinkle the sole skewers with semolina flour, and fry. When cooked, sprinkle with the remaining lemon juice. Serve on dinner plates with herb bouquets.

Wine
Pairings

vegetables

Eggplant Chunks
Browned in Yogurt

Serves 6
- 6 very fresh medium eggplants, peeled and cut into ½-inch cubes
- salt • extra virgin olive oil • 1 garlic clove • freshly ground black pepper
- heaping ½ cup yogurt, drained

Lightly salt the eggplant and place between two kitchen or paper towels for half an hour to allow the salt to draw out some of the water. In a medium skillet, heat some olive oil and fry the whole garlic clove. Add the eggplant cubes and sauté until they are an even golden color. Add salt and pepper and remove from the heat. Finally, remove the garlic clove and stir in the yogurt and a drizzle of olive oil.

Wine
Pairings

Sweet Pepper Timbale

with Yogurt, Sweet Garlic and Watercress Cream

Serves 6

For the garlic cream • 4 garlic cloves • 2¼ cups milk • 1½ cups watercress • salt • ½ cup extra virgin olive oil

For the timbales • 18 oz. red peppers, peeled, seeded, and roughly chopped • heaping ½ cup yogurt, drained • ½ cup ricotta cheese • ¾ cup grated Parmiggiano-Reggiano cheese • salt • freshly ground black pepper • 2 tbsp. egg whites • butter • flour

Preparing the garlic cream Simmer the garlic in the milk for 15 minutes over a low flame. Strain, reserving the garlic and milk, and allow to cool. In the blender, process the cooked garlic cloves, garlic milk, watercress, and salt, adding the oil in a slow stream until creamy.

Preparing the timbales Preheat the oven to 80°F. Process the peppers in a blender; add the yogurt, ricotta, and Parmiggiano-Reggiano. Mix gently and salt and pepper the mixture. Whip the egg whites until stiff and fold gently into the pepper mixture. Now fill six buttered and floured timbale molds with the mixture and place the molds in a baking pan with high sides. Carefully fill the baking pan with hot water until it reaches halfway up the sides of the timbale molds. Place the baking pan with the timbales in the oven and cook for approximately 18 minutes. Unmold the timbales on each plate and serve with the warm garlic watercress cream.

Wine
Pairings

Green Beans
with Sesame, Scallions, and Yogurt

Serves 6
- 2 lbs. green beans • 1 bunch chives • extra virgin olive oil
- 6 scallions, julienned • ½ cup sesame seeds, divided in half
- 1 tsp. mustard • 1 splash white wine • 2 tsp. soy sauce
- salt • freshly ground white pepper • 2 tbsp. yogurt, drained

Blanch the green beans in boiling water, but leave them quite crunchy. Drain, and place in ice water for about 30 seconds. Cut the beans into equal lengths and divide into 18 groups. Tie each group with one or more chives. In a small skillet, add the oil and heat over medium-high. Add the scallions and sauté for 2 minutes. Then add half of the sesame seeds, the mustard, wine, and soy sauce. Heat slowly until the mixture reaches the first signs of boiling. Turn off the heat and season with salt and pepper. Serve the warm beans on dinner plates and drizzle with the scallion sauce, yogurt, and the remaining sesame seeds. Finish with a drizzle of olive oil.

Wine
Pairings

Sardinian Stuffed Tomatoes
with Cream of Yogurt
and Fresh Goat's Milk Cheese

Serves 6
- 18 cherry tomatoes, not overripe • salt • 3½ oz. soft fresh goat cheese
- 2 oz. mascarpone cheese • ¼ cup yogurt, drained • 1 egg white
- a few sprigs of thyme, some leaves removed, plus some stalks reserved for garnish • freshly ground white pepper
- extra virgin olive oil • a few sprigs of tarragon, some finely chopped, plus some stalks reserved for garnish

Wash the tomatoes under very cold running water. Slice off their tops and remove the seeds. Salt lightly. In the meantime, combine the goat and mascarpone cheeses in a bowl with the yogurt, egg white, a few thyme leaves, salt, pepper, a little olive oil, and tarragon. Mix well. Fill the tomatoes completely and arrange them on a lightly oiled baking sheet. Heat the oven to 475°F and cook for 2 – 3 minutes. Garnish with the remaining sprigs of thyme and tarragon; serve.

Wine
Pairings

Jerusalem Artichokes
Au Gratin with Yogurt and Bagos Cheese

Serves 6
- 12 uniformly sized Jerusalem artichokes • 3½ oz. grated Bagos cheese
- ¼ cup yogurt • 2 egg yolks • salt • cayenne pepper • extra virgin olive oil

Boil the Jerusalem artichokes in salted water until cooked. In a bowl, use a wooden spoon to mix the grated cheese, yogurt, egg yolks, salt, and pepper with a little extra virgin olive oil. When the artichokes are cooked, open them halfway, lengthwise, and wrap in aluminum foil, keeping them open. Place in a baking pan and sprinkle the centers with the cheese mixture. Heat the oven to 425°F and cook the artichokes au gratin for about 6 minutes. Serve.

Wine
Pairings

sauces

Eggplant and Yogurt Sauce

Serves 6
- 3 medium eggplants, peeled • extra virgin olive oil for cooking plus 3 tbsp. for the sauce
- 1 garlic clove • salt • freshly ground black pepper • ground ginger
- 1 tbsp. white wine vinegar • heaping ½ cup yogurt, drained

B oil the eggplants in a large pot of lightly salted water. Drain, squeeze, and process in a blender. In a pan, heat the oil, brown the garlic, and add the eggplant purée. Add salt and pepper and remove from heat. Add a pinch of ginger and the 3 tablespoons of olive oil, and blend on low speed. Add the white wine vinegar and the yogurt in a slow stream. This sauce is ideal for toasted breads or as a fresh vegetable dip.

Yogurt and Walnut
Dressing for Summer Salads

Serves 6
- ⅔ cup low-fat yogurt • 3 oz. shelled walnuts • 3 tbsp. extra virgin olive oil
- 1 small hot pepper • ground ginger • fresh juice of 1 lemon. strained
- 1 splash red wine vinegar • salt • 1 bunch chives, minced

In a blender, process the yogurt with the walnuts, oil, pepper, ginger, and lemon juice. Stir in the splash of red wine vinegar, salt, and chives.

Sauce for Grilled Meats

Serves 6
- 1 red pepper • extra virgin olive oil for cooking, plus additional for the sauce
- 1 white onion, chopped • 2 garlic cloves • ¼ cup yogurt, drained
- fresh juice of ½ lemon, strained • 1 tbsp. apple cider vinegar • salt
- cayenne pepper

Blanch the pepper in boiling water, shock in ice water for a few seconds, peel, and roughly chop. Then heat the oil in a skillet and sauté the pepper with the onion and the garlic. Allow to cool, then process the mixture in a blender with the yogurt, lemon, vinegar, salt, cayenne, and extra virgin olive oil until smooth, at least 15 minutes. Serve.

Sauce for Fish

Serves 6
- 3 medium avocados, peeled and chopped • 1 white onion, chopped
- 1 small garlic clove • ¼ cup yogurt, drained • fresh juice of ½ lemon, strained
- 1 small hot pepper • salt • extra virgin olive oil

Process all the ingredients in a blender until a smooth, even paste forms. Serve with fish.

Sauce for Vegetables
Grilled or Steamed

Serves 6
- ½ cup raspberries • ⅓ cup water • ½ cup yogurt, drained
- 2 tbsp. raspberry vinegar • salt • extra virgin olive oil
- 1 bunch chives, finely chopped • 1 bunch tarragon, finely chopped
- a few thyme leaves

In a pan, scald the raspberries in ⅓ cup of simmering water for approximately 3 minutes over a low flame. Allow to cool, process the entire mixture in a blender, and strain. Return the mixture to the blender and add the yogurt, raspberry vinegar, salt, and olive oil. Process until smooth. Pour the sauce into a bowl and add the chives, tarragon, and thyme leaves. Leave to sit for approximately 2 hours. Serve.

bread

White Bread
with Yogurt and Oats

Serves 6

- ⅓ cup plus 1 tbsp. whole milk • 1 heaping tbsp. sugar
- 2½ tbsp. dried (not rapid rise) yeast • 3⅓ lbs. all-purpose or bread flour
- ⅔ cup yogurt, drained and at room temperature • 3 tbsp. salt
- 1½ cups oats • water as needed

W arm the milk, add the sugar and yeast to dissolve, and allow to sit for 10 minutes (the mixture should bubble a bit). In a large bowl, add the milk-sugar mixture and mix with the flour, yogurt, salt, oats, and enough water to form a non-sticky, yet sufficiently moist dough. Turn out onto a surface lightly dusted with flour and knead for approximately 20 minutes. Place in a greased bowl, cover with a damp towel, and let rise in a warm, draft-free place until doubled in size, about 2 hours. Punch down the dough and immediately shape the loaves you want. Cover with a damp towel and let rise again for an hour and a half, then bake at 375°F for 40 minutes.

Focaccia
with Yogurt and Garlic

Serves 6
- 10 oz. pizza dough • scant ¼ cup yogurt, drained
- ¼ cup extra virgin olive oil • salt • 2 garlic cloves, minced
- 1 sprig rosemary for garnish

On a baking sheet, roll the dough out a little less than a half-inch thick. Brush with the yogurt and the olive oil. Sprinkle with salt and garlic. Leave to sit for 10 minutes, then bake in an oven preheated to 400°F for 3 to 4 minutes. Serve, garnishing with the rosemary sprig.

Tin-Loaf Bread
with Yogurt

Serves 6
- 4 cups all purpose or bread flour • 3 tbsp. dry rapid rise yeast
- ¼ cup butter, melted plus additional for greasing • ¾ cup whole milk, warmed
- ⅓ cup yogurt, drained and at room temperature • water • salt

Combine all the dry ingredients in a standing mixer and knead on low speed. Add butter, milk, and yogurt and knead. Butter a bread tin and dust evenly with flour. Place the dough in the tin, cover with a damp towel, and leave to rise at room temperature (68 – 72°F) until it has doubled in volume. Heat the oven to 350°F and bake for approximately 40 minutes.

Bread with Yogurt
and Poppy Seeds

Serves 6
- 1¼ cups water, warm • 2 heaping tbsp. salt • 5 tsp. dry (not rapid rise) yeast
- ¾ cup yogurt, drained • 1⅔ cups all purpose or bread flour
- 1⅔ cups whole-wheat flour • 1¼ cups cereal flour
- 1 heaping tbsp. ground poppy seeds

In the water, dissolve the salt and yeast. Then add the remaining ingredients and knead until the dough is smooth. Cover with a damp cloth and leave to rise for 40 minutes. Shape the loaves you want, cover with a damp towel, and let rise for another hour and 10 minutes. Bake at 375°F for about 40 minutes.

desserts

Ring-Shaped Cookies
with Coffee and Yogurt

Serves 6
- 2¼ cups pastry flour • ¾ cup butter, cold and cubed • ⅓ cup sugar
- 1 packet (3 rounded tsp.) vanilla sugar (or 2 rounded tsp. sugar plus 1 tsp. vanilla extract)
- ¾ cup finely chopped almonds • ½ cup instant coffee granules • 2 tbsp. yogurt, drained
- powdered sugar for dusting

Sift the flour directly onto your work surface. Add the butter, and cut it into the flour with a knife until the mixture is smooth. Add the sugar, vanilla sugar, almonds, coffee, and yogurt. Work it slowly and gently to get a smooth, even dough. Let the dough sit for half an hour. Roll out on a lightly floured surface, cut into 3-inch strips, and gently form into ring shapes. Place on parchment paper and bake in a preheated oven at 340°F for 5 minutes. Dust with powdered sugar before serving.

Wine
Pairings

Frozen Mezzelune
with Yogurt, White Chocolate, and Saffron Threads in a Soup of Chocolate and Coffee with Sweet Croutons

Serves 6

For the mezzelune (half moons) • ¾ cup powdered sugar
• 3 tbsp. fresh pasteurized egg yolks • scant ½ cup yogurt, drained
• 1 pint heavy cream, divided • 2½ oz. white chocolate shavings • 15 threads saffron

For the soup • 1 cup sugar • 1⅓ cups water • 2 cups cocoa (not Dutch process)
• ⅓ cup instant coffee granules • 1 tbsp. plus 1 tsp. butter
• 4 slices sweet bread (such as brioche), cubed

Preparing the mezzelune In a saucepan, whisk the sugar and egg yolks thoroughly. Add the yogurt and continue whisking until the mixture is smooth and homogenous. In another bowl, whip 1½ cups of the cream until soft peaks form. Bring a few inches of water to a simmer in a saucepot. Place the chocolate in a bowl that will fit comfortably on top of the pot. Set the bowl over the simmering water and stir the chocolate until it melts. Let cool for about 1 minute. Add the remaining ½ cup of non-whipped cream to the melted chocolate. Delicately blend the egg and chocolate mixtures together, and then fold in the whipped cream and the saffron. Fill crescent-shaped molds and place them in the freezer for at least 6 hours.

Preparing the soup Simmer the sugar, water, and cocoa over a low flame, mixing carefully for 8 – 10 minutes. Add the coffee, and then allow to cool.

Preparing the croutons Melt the butter in a pan over medium heat, add the bread, and sauté until crunchy.

Plating Pour the soup into bowls. Top each portion with an iced mezzelune, and finish with the sweet croutons.

Wine Pairings

Yogurt and Nougat Flutes
with Dark Chocolate Shavings

Serves 6
- 1 pint heavy cream, divided • scant ½ cup yogurt, drained • ⅓ cup sugar
- 2 egg yolks • ¹⁄₁₀ oz. powdered gelatin (a bit more than ⅓ of a packet)
- 3½ oz. nougat, chopped • 2 oz. dark chocolate

For optional garnish • 6 fresh strawberries • 6 mint sprigs

In a bowl, lightly whip 1⅔ cups cream to soft peaks. In a second bowl, use an electric mixer to beat the yogurt, sugar, and egg yolks until well integrated. In the meantime, sprinkle the gelatin over a small amount of cold water to soften. Let sit for 3 – 5 minutes without mixing, until it swells. In a saucepot, warm the remaining ⅓ cup cream to 200°F and in it, dissolve the nougat. Remove from the heat. When the cream-nougat liquid reduces in temperature to 150°F, squeeze the water out of the gelatin and let it dissolve in the cream-nougat mixture. Combine the nougat and yogurt-egg mixtures, stirring vigorously with a whisk. Gently fold in the whipped cream and pour into long-stemmed champagne glasses. Leave the glasses in the refrigerator for about 2 hours. Before serving, use a grater with large holes to grate room temperature chocolate into shavings on top. Garnish with fresh strawberries and mint leaves.

Wine
Pairings

Fried Gianduiotti
with Yogurt

Serves 6

For the centers • 6½ oz. dark or milk chocolate, chopped
• ⅓ cup plus 1 tbsp. yogurt, drained • ¼ cup powdered sugar
• ⅓ cup cocoa powder (not Dutch process)

For the batter • 2 eggs • 3 tbsp. rum • 1 packet (3 rounded tsp.) vanilla
   sugar (or 2 rounded tsp. sugar plus 1 tsp. vanilla extract) • 1 pinch salt
• ½ cup milk • ½ cup flour

For frying and serving • 2 quarts peanut oil • powdered sugar for sprinkling

Preparing the gianduiotti centers Bring a few inches of water to a simmer in a saucepot. Place the chocolate in a bowl that will fit comfortably over the pot and set the pot over the simmering water. Stir until the chocolate melts. Remove from the heat and add the yogurt, powdered sugar, and cocoa, stirring with a whisk. Allow to cool and shape the gianduiotti with two teaspoons, like making quenelles, and place them on a rack covered with wax paper. Leave in the freezer at least overnight.

Preparing the gianduiotti batter In a bowl, whisk together the eggs, rum, vanilla sugar, salt, and milk. Add the flour in a continuous stream, whisking constantly and making sure there are no lumps. Cover with plastic wrap and refrigerate for 2 – 3 hours.

Frying and serving Remove the well-frozen gianduiotti from the freezer (a few at a time) and dip them in the very cold batter. Immediately fry them in the peanut oil, preheated to 350°F. Remove from the oil with a skimmer, drain on paper towels, and serve immediately, sprinkling with powdered sugar.

Wine
Pairings

Puff Pastry Napoleons

*with Lemon Cream Yogurt
and Tropical Fruit Sauce*

Serves 6

For the lemon cream yogurt • 2 cups milk • 3 egg yolks • ½ cup sugar • ¼ cup flour • 2½ tbsp. cornstarch • freshly grated zest of 1 lemon • ⅓ cup lemon yogurt, drained

For the tropical fruit sauce • ¾ cup water • ¼ cup sugar • 10 oz. fresh pineapple, flesh cubed • 1 orange, flesh cubed • 1 pink grapefruit, flesh cubed • 1 papaya, flesh cubed • 1 kiwi, flesh cubed • 1 star fruit, sliced • ½ cup dry white wine • fresh juice of 1 lemon, strained

For the presentation and optional garnish • 12 baked 3 × 3-inch puff pastry squares • additional fresh fruit cubes • lemon balm sprigs

Preparing the lemon cream yogurt In a medium saucepot, heat the milk to 175°F. In a bowl, mix the egg yolks, sugar, flour, cornstarch, and zest with a whisk, making sure there are no lumps. Pour the hot milk directly into the egg mixture, stirring vigorously and constantly with a whisk. Pour everything back into the pot and heat to 195°F, still stirring constantly. Remove the pan from the heat, strain the mixture into a bowl if necessary, and cover with plastic wrap. Allow to cool. Then fold in the yogurt.

Preparing the tropical fruit sauce Place the water and sugar in a small saucepot. Simmer for about 2 minutes until the sugar dissolves. Cool. Place the fruit in a bowl and mix with 2½ tbsp. of the sugar syrup, the wine, and the lemon juice. (Reserve the remaining light sugar syrup for another use.) Then chill the sauce for about 2 hours in the refrigerator.

Plating Spoon some tropical fruit sauce into each soup plate, followed by one square of puff pastry. Spoon some lemon cream yogurt over the square and top with another puff pastry square. Repeat with all six servings, garnishing with a few fruit cubes and lemon balm sprigs.

Wine
Pairings

LE CONCHE
**PASSITO
DI PANTELLERIA**
IMBOTTIGLIATO NELL'ISOLA

Soft Yogurt "Dumplings"

Drenched in Red Berry Sauce
with Lingue di Gatto

Serves 6

***For the* lingue di gatto** *(cats' tongues)* • 7 tbsp. butter, cubed and at room temperature • 1 cup sifted powdered sugar • 3½ oz. egg whites • 1 cup sifted white flour

For the red berry sauce • 18 oz. berries (strawberries, raspberries, currants, blackberries, blueberries), divided • 1 cup sugar • 2 tbsp. fresh lemon juice, strained

For the dumplings • 6 gelatin leaves • 3½ cups heavy cream, scant ½ cup warmed • 2 egg yolks • ½ cup sugar • 1 scant cup yogurt, drained

For the optional garnish • 18 fresh mint leaves

Preparing the *lingue di gatto* Cream the butter and sugar with an electric mixer, then mix in the egg whites a bit at a time. Slowly add the sifted flour and beat until smooth. Spread the dough on a parchment-lined baking sheet in the desired shape ("cats' tongues"), and bake at 400°F for 3 minutes.

Preparing the sauce In a small pot, boil 10 oz. of the berries with the sugar and the lemon juice for about 5 minutes. Strain, if desired, and set aside.

Preparing the dumplings Soak the gelatin leaves in cold water until soft. Squeeze and dissolve in the warmed scant half cup of cream, stirring occasionally until clear. In a saucepan, beat the egg yolks and sugar and blend in the yogurt and gelatin-cream mixture. In another bowl, whip the remaining cream and slowly fold it into the egg-yogurt mixture. When the consistency is smooth, put it in a container to chill in the refrigerator for at least 2 hours. With two large spoons, shape the dumplings into quenelles and serve them on flat plates, pouring the berry sauce over the top and garnishing with the *lingue di gatto* and the mint leaves.

Wine
Pairings

Chocolate Millefoglie
with Yogurt and Passionfruit Mousse

Serves 6

For the chocolate squares • 9 oz. dark chocolate (70%)
• 1 oz. cocoa (not Dutch process), sifted
For the mousse • 2 gelatin leaves • 1 pint heavy cream, 1½ cups plus
   1 tbsp. whipped to soft peaks and the remaining scant ½ cup at room temperature
• pulp from 4 passionfruit • ½ cup plus 1 tbsp. sugar • scant ½ cup yogurt, drained
For the garnish • pulp from 3 passionfruit • 6 lemon balm sprigs

Preparing the chocolate squares Bring a few inches of water to a simmer in a saucepot. Place chocolate in a bowl that will sit comfortably on top of the pot. Place the bowl on top of the pot and stir the chocolate until it melts. Once it melts, keep the water simmering. Remove from heat and blend the cocoa into the melted chocolate. Spread the mixture on a baking sheet and allow to cool for a few minutes. Cut the chocolate into 1½-inch squares.

Preparing the mousse Soak the gelatin leaves in cold water until soft. Squeeze and dissolve in the room temperature cream in a bowl set over the pan of simmering water. Stir until the gelatin is incorporated. Meanwhile, heat the pulp of four passionfruit in a saucepan with the sugar over a low flame for about 3 minutes, then strain the mixture. Add the cream-gelatin mixture to the passionfruit mixture with the yogurt and the whipped cream. Place in the refrigerator for at least half an hour.

Plating To serve, place one chocolate square on each plate. Using a pastry bag with a star-shaped tube, pipe the yogurt and passion fruit mousse in the center. Top with another chocolate square, followed by more mousse and a final chocolate square, thus creating the "millefoglie." Garnish with the remaining passionfruit pulp and lemon balm.

Wine
Pairings

Crunchy Yogurt
and Sesame Strips

Serves 6
- 3½ oz. egg whites • ⅓ cup sugar • 1½ cups yogurt, drained
- 1 pinch salt • 1 scant cup flour • ⅓ cup sesame seeds, divided
- ⅓ cup butter, melted and cooled to room temperature

Beat the egg whites with the sugar, yogurt, and salt in a standing mixer. Add the flour in portions along with ⅔ of the sesame seeds. Slowly pour in the melted butter and continue mixing until the mixture is smooth and shiny. With a pastry tube, pipe the dough in strips onto a baking sheet lined with parchment paper and sprinkle with the remaining sesame seeds. Bake in a preheated oven at 375°F for 6 – 7 minutes.

Wine
Pairings

Soft Yogurt
and Chocolate Drops

Serves 6
- 2 egg whites • ¾ cup flour • 1 cup slivered almonds
- 2½ tsp. baking powder • heaping ⅓ cup sugar • ⅓ cup yogurt, drained
- 3½ oz. dark chocolate chips

Whip the egg whites until they form stiff peaks. In a second bowl, mix the flour with the almonds and yeast. Add the sugar little by little to the egg whites without stopping the mixer. Now very slowly, while continuing to mix, add the flour mixture to the egg white mixture. By hand, fold in the yogurt and chocolate chips. Use a dessert spoon to shape the drops and place on a parchment paper–lined baking sheet. Bake at 400°F for about 6 – 8 minutes. Allow to cool, and serve.

Wine
Pairings

Banana and Yogurt Mousse
with a Tangerine Reduction

Serves 6

For the tangerine reduction • juice of 3 tangerines, strained
• 1 oz. pectin • 2 tbsp. powdered sugar • 2 cups tangerine liqueur
For the mousse • ⅔ cup banana cubes • fresh juice of ½ lemon, strained
• 1½ gelatin leaves • 1½ cups heavy cream, divided
• ⅓ cup yogurt, drained • scant ½ cup sugar • 2 egg yolks
For optional garnish • fresh fruit

Preparing the tangerine reduction In a small saucepan, combine the tangerine reduction ingredients and bring to a simmer over a low flame, whisking for 3 – 4 minutes. Allow to cool before serving.

Preparing the mousse In a blender, process the banana and lemon juice into a smooth purée. Pour into a medium bowl. Put the gelatin in cold water to soften. With an electric mixer, whip 1¼ cups of the cream to soft peaks. Pour remaining ¼ cup of cream in a saucepan and heat to 150°F. To the banana purée, add the yogurt, sugar, and egg yolks, mixing well with a whisk. Squeeze the water out of the gelatin and dissolve it in the hot cream. Add the gelatin-cream mixture to the banana mixture, whisking well. Delicately fold in the semi-whipped cream. Pour into a bowl, cover with plastic wrap, and place in the refrigerator for at least 2 hours. Use two spoons to shape the mousse into quenelles and arrange on dinner plates. Garnish with a bit of fresh fruit and the tangerine reduction.

Wine
Pairings

Sponge Cake
with Yogurt, Hazelnuts, and Chocolate

Serves 6

- 2 sticks butter, cubed • 1½ cups sugar • ¾ cup plus 1 tbsp. whole eggs
- 1 scant cup yogurt, drained • ¼ cup whole milk • 2½ cups flour • ¾ cup potato starch
- 1 tbsp. plus 1 tsp. yeast for desserts • ¾ cup finely chopped hazelnuts
- 2½ oz. chocolate chips • pinch salt

In a standing mixer, whip the butter with the sugar at medium speed. Once they're well mixed, add the eggs in a stream, with the mixer running slowly. Now add the yogurt and milk and blend steadily. In a bowl, sift the flour with the starch and yeast and carefully incorporate these dry ingredients into the wet mixture. Then carefully blend in the hazelnuts, chocolate chips, and salt. Pour the mixture into two 8-inch cake tins. Heat the oven to 350°F and bake the sponge cakes for about 20 minutes.

Wine
Pairings

Chestnut and Yogurt Truffles

Serves 6
- 3⅓ cups whole milk • 1 vanilla bean pod, halved vertically, seeds removed and both seeds and pod reserved • 10 oz. shelled and peeled chestnuts
- 1¼ oz. pectin • ½ cup sugar • ¼ cup yogurt, drained • 1 packet (3 rounded tsp.) vanilla sugar (or 2 rounded tsp. sugar plus 1 tsp. vanilla extract)
- 2 tbsp. rum • 1 cup cocoa powder (not Dutch-process)

In a small pot, bring the milk to a boil with the vanilla pod and seeds. Add the nuts and boil until they fall apart and the milk is completely absorbed. Remove the vanilla pod and discard. Press the warm chestnuts through a ricer and combine with the pectin, sugar, yogurt, vanilla sugar, and rum. Shape into ½-inch balls and roll in cocoa. Serve the truffles in special paper cups.

Wine
Pairings

Orange Chocolate Balls
with Dried Fruit and Yogurt

Serves 6
- 2 oz. dried figs • 2 oz. pitted dates • 3 oz. chopped almonds
- 3 oz. chopped hazelnuts • 2½ oz. yogurt • ¼ cup brown sugar • ¼ cup sugar
- 1 oz. pectin • ⅓ cup fresh orange juice, strained • 7 oz. dark chocolate (70%), chopped
- ⅓ cup cocoa powder (not Dutch process)

Process the figs and dates in a blender. In a bowl, mix the almonds, hazelnuts, yogurt, sugars, and pectin. Use a wooden spoon to combine the puréed dried fruit and the orange juice and mix well with the nut-sugar mixture. Form ½-inch balls with your hands. Bring a few inches of water to a simmer in a saucepot. Place the chocolate in a bowl that will fit comfortably on top of the pot. Place the bowl on the pot and stir the chocolate until it melts. Add the cocoa to the melted chocolate and stir well. Roll the balls in the chocolate mixture and set them on a plate. Leave to harden and then place the sweets in special praline cups.

Wine Pairings

Chilled Yogurt
and Chestnut Honey Dessert
with Sugared Chestnuts and Milk Chocolate Sauce

Serves 6

For the yogurt honey cream • 2 cups plus 2 tbsp. heavy cream
• ⅓ cup sugar • 3 tbsp. chestnut honey • 2 egg yolks • ⅓ cup yogurt, drained

For the sugared chestnuts • 10 oz. shelled and peeled chestnuts
• ¼ cup brown sugar, packed • ½ cup sugar • 5 tbsp. water

For the chocolate sauce • 5 oz. milk chocolate, chopped • 1¼ cups heavy cream
• 1 splash crème de cocoa

Preparing the yogurt honey cream With a standing or electric mixer, whip 1¾ cups of cream to medium peaks. In a second bowl, whisk the sugar, honey, and egg yolks, and add the yogurt in a stream. Prepare custard molds, wetted slightly with cold water. Gently fold the whipped cream into the yogurt and honey mixture, add the remaining cream (not whipped), and pour evenly into the molds. Cover and refrigerate at least 4 hours.

Preparing the sugared chestnuts Parboil the chestnuts in lightly salted water, keeping them whole. Remove, drain, and set aside. Pour the two sugars into a small to medium pot over a low-medium flame and stir often until they turn a light hazelnut color. Remove from the heat and immediately stir in the water. Then immediately add the chestnuts to the caramel, and toss carefully. Set aside.

Preparing the chocolate sauce Bring a few inches of water to a simmer in a saucepot. Place the chocolate in a bowl that will fit comfortably on top of the pot. Place the bowl on top of the pot and stir until the chocolate melts. Add the 1¼ cups cream and cocoa cream, mixing with a whisk.

Plating Serve the creams chilled in their molds, garnished with the sugared chestnuts and a spoonful of chocolate sauce.

Wine
Pairings

Fruit Stew

with Star Anise and Green Pepper, and Mint-Flavored Yogurt Gelato

Serves 6

For the fruit stew • ¼ cup sugar • ¾ cup water
• 1 lb. 5 oz. mixed fresh fruit in cubes, such as strawberries and pineapple
• 12 star anise pods • ½ oz. dry green pepper • 6 – 7 fresh mint leaves
• 6 – 7 lemon balm leaves

For the mint-flavored yogurt gelato • 2¼ cups whole milk
• ⅓ cup low-fat milk powder • 10 fresh mint leaves • ⅓ cup egg yolks
• ¾ cup plus 1 tbsp. sugar • 1 oz. apricot jam • ½ cup yogurt, drained

In a small saucepot, combine the sugar and water and simmer for 2 minutes until the sugar dissolves. Set aside. Combine ¼ cup of this syrup (reserve the remaining syrup for another use), plus all of the other fruit stew ingredients in a bowl, cover, and marinate at least overnight. In a small saucepan, heat the whole and powdered milk and mint leaves to 175°F. In a bowl, whisk together the egg yolks with the sugar and jam. Combine the milk-mint and egg-sugar mixtures, straining out the mint, and cool to 85°F. Now mix in the yogurt, cover, and return to the refrigerator for 6 – 7 hours. Freeze in an ice cream maker, following the manufacturer's instructions. Serve the stew in dessert bowls or soup plates, placing a scoop of mint-flavored yogurt gelato in the middle.

Wine
Pairings

Banana Yogurt Cake

Serves 6
- 1 stick minus 1 tbsp. butter, at room temperature • ⅔ cup sugar
- 3 eggs, yolks and whites separated • scant ⅔ cup banana yogurt, drained
- heaping ½ cup semolina flour, sifted • ¾ cup white flour, sifted
- 1 packet of yeast powder for desserts • 1 medium banana, cubed

In a standing or electric mixer, cream the butter and sugar and add the three egg yolks one at a time, continuing to whisk. Add the yogurt slowly, followed by the sifted flours and yeast. In another bowl, beat the three egg whites until fluffy. Add the bananas, and finally the beaten egg whites to the batter and pour into a buttered and floured 10-inch cake pan. Bake at 400°F for about 45 minutes.

Wine
Pairings

Soft Yogurt Cake
with Strawberries and Prosecco

Serves 6

For strawberry yogurt filling • 1½ pints fresh strawberries, trimmed and hulled
• water • 1 prebaked 12-inch cookie dough or graham cracker crust
• 3½ cups heavy cream, divided • heaping ½ cup yogurt • ¾ cup plus 2 tbsp. sugar
• 2 egg yolks • ½ oz. powdered gelatin • fresh fruit for garnish
For the Prosecco gelatin • ⅕ oz. powdered gelatin • 2 cups Prosecco
• ⅓ cup plus 1 tbsp. sugar

Preparing the strawberry yogurt filling In a blender, purée the strawberries with enough water to make 1⅓ cups of juice. Leave the crust in its original tin, and wrap it with a strip of acetate. With a standing or electric mixer, whip 3 cups plus 2 tablespoons of cream to soft peaks. In a second bowl, whisk the yogurt, sugar, 1 cup plus 1 tablespoon strawberry juice, and egg yolks until the mixture is creamy. In another small bowl, sprinkle the gelatin over a small amount of cold water and set aside for 3 – 5 minutes without stirring, until the mixture swells. In a small saucepan, warm the remaining 6 tablespoons of cream to 150°F. Squeeze out the water from the gelatin and dissolve it in the warmed cream, whisking well. Pour the gelatin mixture into the strawberry-yogurt mixture and stir. Gently fold in the whipped cream and pour the mixture into the cookie crust. Place in the refrigerator for 2 hours.

Preparing the Prosecco gelatin Sprinkle the gelatin over a small amount of cold water and set aside for 3 – 5 minutes without stirring, until the mixture swells. Warm the Prosecco with the sugar in a small pan to 150°F. Squeeze out the water and dissolve the gelatin mixture in the Prosecco liquid. Add ¼ cup of the remaining strawberry juice and stir. Allow to cool.

Assembling Remove the cake from the refrigerator and pour the Prosecco jelly on top before it congeals. Return the cake to the refrigerator and wait for the jelly to set completely, about half an hour. Gently remove the cake from the tin, remove the acetate sheet, and garnish with fresh fruit.

Wine
Pairings

Yogurt and Aphrodite

by Mario Busso

Since antiquity, humankind has searched for systems and substances that would amplify the amorous abilities, placing special importance on food. Aphrodisiac foods are mentioned in Egyptian medical papyri and the Bible: "Your lips distil nectar, my bride; honey and milk are under your tongue; the scent of your garments is like the scent of Lebanon" (Solomon in the Song of Solomon). All the great Greek and Latin poets sang the praises of this or that food deemed able to elevate the amorous virtues. In *The Art of Love*, Ovid lauded the aphrodisiac action of arugula—aphrodisiac eruca herb—that grew spontaneously around the phallic statues dedicated to Priapus. To increase the sex drive, the Greeks suggested onions, carrots, truffles, honey, eggs, fish, and crustaceans; the last above all, because they come from the sea, which gave birth to Aphrodite, the goddess of love. The Romans extended this list to include the genital organs of certain animals, but reserved their highest esteem for oysters. In the Middle Ages, people swore by the aphrodisiac effect of pigeon brains, and later, the fiery Catherine of Forlì lauded extract of dried donkey penis, aligning herself with Oriental beliefs, certain of the powers of rhinoceros horn, shark fins, and tiger testicles.

Although many of those items—like oysters, fish, spices, truffles, and chocolate—contain glycogen, phosphorus, phenylethylamine, and androstenediol, and some fruits—such as hot peppers—cause vasodilation in the lumbosacral area that includes the genitals, I personally am nearly certain that true aphrodisiac foods do not exist. Situations elevate them to this function. As the greatest expert in "immoral recipes," Manuel Vázquez Montalbán, said, "We know of no one who has succeeded in seduction through what that person offered to eat; there is, however, a long list of those who have seduced by describing what was about to be eaten." Aphrodisiac foods or ingredients do not satiate, they are allusive ingredients that rouse the appetite of the spirit. Love and passion are born of seduction, and even though here we enter the realm of subjectivity, among amorous strategies, those that involve the kitchen stove or a table in an intimate restaurant appear to rank among the most successful. It is in that precise instant that someone decides to take a step forward or backward that everything happens through the language of food. Appetite and flavor are good indicators of feelings and emotions, because nourishing and accepting nourishment reproduce that deep and unique bond upon which depends such a large part of our being, our fears and pleasures, a bond that is perpetuated in the psychological imagination as game-dependence between mother and child. Eating is indubitably a fact of culture and coding; to an equal degree so are love, falling in love, and seduction. In all of this we feel the natural need to communicate and to experience according to the models and perceptions of our emotional state and our cultural ability to express ourselves in the most elevated spheres.

But what does aphrodisiac cooking have to do with all of this? The easy answer is in the adjective. Aphrodite, the Greek goddess of love, in exchange for an apple urged Helen, the most beautiful of the Achaeans, into the arms of Paris. Therefore, "aphrodisiac" is that which makes us fall in love and rouses passion, that which leads two people to hide themselves away and leave the world outside the door. Only then, I confess, can the intrigue of aromas and flavors of certain recipes spark delicious thoughts, irresistible impulses, perverse and transporting bursts of imagination: only then can foods draw the mind toward secret longings and build a bridge between appetite and lust. Eroticism and sexual love are therefore inseparable from food, because enjoyment of food—Isabel Allende suggests—is a road leading directly to lust and, if followed overindulgently, to the perdition of the soul. This is why Lutherans, Calvinists, and others aspiring to Christian perfection eat poorly. Catholics however, who are born resigned to original sin and human weakness, and who, thanks to the sacrament of confession, return pure and ready to sin again, are therefore so flexible in regards to food that they even coined the expression "the priest's mouthful" to describe the most delicious dishes. It was precisely for this reason that the Marquis de Sade, master of desecration, attributed to these sacred morsels the ability to produce voluptuous sensations. But food and love also coexist because their stories have been supported for centuries by popular tradition. The language of love and that of food overlap each other constantly: the hair of a lover flows like a field of grain moved by the breeze; her eyes are almond-shaped and the color of hazelnuts; her skin is velvety as a peach; her lips are cherry red, their shape is appetizing. The ambiguity of the gastro-amorous language continues into figures of speech. The French call their beloved "mon petit chou"—my little cabbage; Americans use the word "cookie" for their girlfriends; the English refer to sexy women as "crumpet," which is a fried, oily type of muffin. The repetition of amorous situations, reduced to the level of habit, becomes banal reheated broth. But the first post-matrimonial period is called the honeymoon, whose symbolism derives from the Roman custom requiring the groom, holding his bride in his arms, to cross his threshold, covered in honey, without slipping. The only preservative known in antiquity, honey was an allegory for the lengthy union of the newlyweds.

From here, it's quite a leap to say that yogurt in cooking can become an accomplice to seduction. Indeed, if yogurt represents lightness to dieters, it often also assumes a restrictive, flavor-inhibitive nature. All of these characteristics distance food from its hedonistic function, and tend to preclude the path that may extend from the kitchen towards the nuptial bed. To shatter this conception, in the recipes we present here, yogurt works shoulder to shoulder with other ingredients to sharpen Cupid's arrows. Precisely because it is light and replaces fats, it leaves the mind fresh and avoids those confused sleepy states that often close the meal, thus helping to raise the humble dishes to the succulence of seduction. They are also supported by the wines, which, skillfully paired with the recipes, as Apuleius said, "defeat the cowardice of modesty to bring pleasure to the fore." The recipes in our aphrodisiac dinner are taken in part from *Aphrodite* by Isabel Allende (Feltrinelli publishers), and in part from the *Cucina dell'Amore*. I recommend them personally, in part because they are simple to make and have been tried and tested in the sequence of their delightful ability to stimulate desire and foreshadow imminent caresses. Just like truffles, oysters, lobsters, and every other "gift from God" considered to be an aphrodisiac, these recipes require soft lighting, background music, and skill in the person describing them to be creative and original, creating mystery and sparking the imagination, exciting desire: a sensation at first imperceptible that slowly becomes as overpowering as a raging river.

Cream of Artichoke Soup

by Isabel Allende (*Aphrodite*, pub. Feltrinelli)

Serves 2

- 2 artichokes
- 1 lemon slice
- 2 cups chicken broth
- 9 oz. yogurt, drained
- salt
- freshly ground black pepper
- 2 tsp. butter

Cook the artichokes in boiling salted water with the lemon until they are tender and the leaves detach easily (30 – 40 minutes). Once cooled, separate the meat from the leaves with a spoon. Use a knife to remove the choke from the hearts. In a blender, purée the meat and stems with the broth and yogurt. Add salt and pepper to taste. Heat and serve with a knob of butter in each bowl.

Wine Pairings

Cream of Peas

by Angelo Troiani (*Convivio Troiani*, Rome)

Serves 2

- 20 fresh mint leaves
- 4 tbsp. extra virgin olive oil
- 28 oz. yogurt, drained
- white, coarse salt to taste
- knob of butter • 10.5 oz. fresh peas
- 2 small shallots, finely chopped
- 1 garlic clove, minced
- 7 oz. Swiss chard leaves
- 6 ladles vegetable broth
- freshly ground black pepper

Place the mint leaves in 3 tbsp. olive oil for a day to infuse. In a bowl, mix the yogurt with coarse salt, wrap in a cloth, and leave to drain in the bowl for a few hours until the yogurt curdles. In a saucepan over a low flame, add a teaspoon of olive oil and a knob of butter, melt the butter, and cook the peas with the shallots and garlic, covered, over low heat, for 10 – 15 minutes. Meanwhile, bring a pot of salted water to a boil and quickly blanch the chard leaves, then transfer immediately to a bowl of ice water. Drain and process the chard in a blender with the pea mixture, and adjust the thickness with vegetable broth. Add salt and pepper to taste. Separate the thickened, drained yogurt from the whey and shape quenelles with a spoon. Pour the warm soup into soup bowls. Arrange three small yogurt quenelles in each bowl, and finish with a drizzle of mint-infused oil. Sprinkle with pepper and serve.

Wine Pairings

Habanero Shrimp

by Isabel Allende (*Aphrodite*, pub. Feltrinelli)

Serves 2

- 1 whole grapefruit
- 1 cup boiled shrimp
- 1 apple, cubed
- 1 tbsp. chopped walnuts
- 2 tbsp. fresh cilantro, chervil, and mint, chopped

For the sauce:

- 2 tbsp. yogurt, drained
- 1 tsp. fresh lemon juice, strained
- 1 tbsp. honey
- pinch mustard
- 1 tbsp. soybean oil
- freshly ground black pepper

Halve the grapefruit. Cut out all of the flesh and cube. Reserve both the flesh cubes and the skin and place in the refrigerator. Mix together the shrimp, grapefruit cubes, apple, nuts, and herbs. Just before serving, whisk together all the sauce ingredients except the oil. Slowly drizzle in the oil, whisking constantly. Season with a little black pepper. Toss the salad with the dressing, and spoon into the two grapefruit halves. Serve.

Wine Pairings

Venus's Eggplant

by Walter Eynard (*Flipot*, Torre Pellice)

Serves 2

- 2 medium eggplants, cut vertically into four pieces
- 2 small-medium garlic cloves, smashed and divided
- 1 tbsp. fresh lemon juice, strained
- sea salt
- freshly ground black pepper
- 2 tbsp. parsley, chopped
- 2 tbsp. olive oil
- 1 cup fresh mushrooms, minced
- ½ red pepper, cut into strips
- ¼ cup tomato sauce
- 1 tbsp. wine grappa
- ¼ cup yogurt, drained

Combine eggplant with half of the garlic, lemon, salt, pepper, and parsley. Allow to sit for an hour, and then grill for 15 minutes. Heat oil in a skillet and sauté the mushrooms with the remaining garlic and the pepper. Add the tomato sauce and the grappa, and cook for 5 minutes. Remove from the heat, and pour the sauce over the grilled eggplant. Serve cold with the yogurt.

Wine Pairings

Fish a la Newborg

by Isabel Allende (*Aphrodite*, pub. Feltrinelli)

Serves 2

- 2 slices or fillets white fish
  (about 12 – 16 ounces)
- 1 tbsp. whiskey • ¼ cup fish broth
- 1 tbsp. butter • ½ cup heavy cream
- ½ cup yogurt, drained • 2 egg yolks
- salt • freshly ground black pepper
- paprika
- ½ tbsp. freshly grated lemon zest

Bring salted water to a bare simmer in a saucepot and add the fish. Poach until cooked through, about 10 minutes, transfer to a plate, and cover with foil to keep warm. Combine the whiskey and the fish broth and set aside. Heat a few inches of water to a simmer in a saucepot. In a bowl that will fit comfortably on top of the pot, add the butter, cream, yogurt, and egg yolks. Whisk well and cook over low heat without boiling, continuing to stir. When the mixture thickens, slowly pour in the whiskey–fish broth mixture, followed by the spices and the lemon zest. Continue whisking over a low flame for another 5 minutes. Adjust seasoning if necessary with salt, and serve with the poached fish.

Wine Pairings

Yogurt Mousse

by Ivan Pinter and Masahiko Jagi (*Rêve Cafè*, Milan)

Serves 2

- 18 oz. fresh vegetables, julienned
- 2 cups yogurt, drained
- salt
- extra virgin olive oil
- cayenne
- fresh mint, chopped
- fresh tarragon, chopped
- fennel, chopped
- 1 green apple, ½ in very small cubes
  and ½ in thin slices with peel for
  garnish, reserved in salted water
- 3 oz. king crab meat

Blanch the vegetables in boiling salted water and shock in ice water. Drain and set aside. Put the yogurt in a piece of cheesecloth with a very tight weave and hang it over a bowl for 6 hours in the refrigerator to eliminate all excess liquid. Then place the condensed yogurt in a bowl and season with salt, oil, and cayenne. At this point, pour the seasoned yogurt into individual bowls, top with the herbs and then the vegetables, and repeat the layering. Combine the crabmeat with the apple cubes, salt, and cayenne. Drain the apple slices. Finish with yogurt and apple slices. Arrange the crab salad alongside. Decorate with additional fresh herbs and season with a drizzle of extra virgin olive oil.

Wine Pairings

Papaya with Yogurt

by Antonio Chiodi Latini (*Nove Merli*, Piossasco)

Serves 2

For the papaya:
- 1 small papaya, peeled and halved, seeds removed
- 1 cup yogurt, drained
- 2 tbsp. fresh lemon juice, strained
- ½ cup honey

For the spiced toasted almonds:
- ½ cup peeled almonds
- scant tsp. curry

Preparing the almonds

Finely chop half a cup of peeled almonds. Toast them until lightly browned in a non-stick pan with a tiny spoonful of curry (add more if you like your almonds very spicy).

Preparing the papaya

Divide the papaya between two plates. Completely cover with the yogurt. Mix the lemon juice with the honey, and then pour over the papaya. Top with the almonds.

Wine Pairings

Slices of Sea Bass

by Giancarlo Guarnieri (*Gustavino*, Florence)

Serves 2
- 20 green beans
- ½ red or green pepper
- ½ celery stalk
- 1 zucchini
- 1 carrot
- 1 artichoke, cut into segments
- extra virgin olive oil
- 1 shallot, minced
- 3 oysters, chopped
- juice of ½ lemon, strained
- scant ½ cup low-fat yogurt, drained
- 4 four-oz. pieces sea bass, boned

Cut vegetables into 4 × ⅛-inch pieces. In slightly acidulous boiling water, blanch the vegetables and transfer to a bowl of salted ice water. Drain and reserve. Heat a bit of oil in a skillet and soften the shallot over medium heat. Add the oysters, lemon juice, and yogurt, and simmer for about 3 minutes. Blend in a food processor and dilute with water to the right consistency. Steam the sea bass, reheat the sauce, and spoon it over each plate. Arrange the vegetables in a checkerboard pattern on top. Finish with the warm sea bass.

Wine Pairings

Yogurt around the World

by Chiara Busso

INDIA
Chicken Tandoori

- 3 chickens, 1 to 1½ lbs. each • 2 cups yogurt, drained • 1 tbsp. chopped papaya
- 6 tbsp. vinegar • 1 tsp. freshly ground black pepper • ½ tsp. ground cayenne
- 2 tsp. chili powder • 2 tbsp. ground ginger • 2 tsp. ground coriander • 2 tsp. ground cumin
- 2 tsp. ground cardamom • 3 tsp. salt • 6 garlic cloves • fresh lemon juice, strained
- 1 stick butter, melted • Optional garnish: thin lemon slices
- Optional garnish: fresh cilantro or parsley leaves

With a very sharp knife, make numerous incisions in the breasts and thighs of the chickens, being careful not to cut the joints (however, the chickens may be halved or quartered if preferred). In a large bowl, mix yogurt, papaya, vinegar, spices, garlic, and lemon juice. Add the chickens, turning to cover them entirely. Leave to marinate for 6 – 7 hours, or overnight. Drain and brush with some of the melted butter. Roast on a grill over a bed of embers, turning and basting with more butter occasionally. Serve warm and garnish with lemon slices and cilantro or parsley.

GREECE
Lamb with Yogurt

- 4½ lbs. lamb • 2 sticks butter, melted • salt • 1 cup water • 3⅓ lbs. yogurt, drained
- freshly ground black pepper • 4 – 5 eggs, whites and yolks separated

Wash and dry the meat thoroughly and place in a roasting pan. Rub with some of the butter and season generously with salt. Pour water and additional butter and salt around the lamb in the pan. Bake at 350°F until fully cooked. In the meantime, mix the yogurt with salt and pepper in a bowl. In another bowl, beat the egg whites. Add the egg yolks, whip together, and pour in the seasoned yogurt, continuing to whisk. Remove the meat from the roasting pan and set aside. Pour the yogurt-egg mixture into the pan juices and stir. Return the pan to the oven and cook until a dense cream is formed. Put the meat back in the pan and leave to allow the flavors to combine. When the color develops, remove from the oven and serve.

PAKISTAN
Biryani

- 2¼ lbs. lamb cubes • ½ cup yogurt • ½ tsp. saffron threads • 1 cup butter • 2 large onions, sliced
- 2½ tbsp. cumin seeds • 2½ tbsp. ground cloves • 2½ tbsp. cinnamon • pinch ground ginger
- 2½ tbsp. cardamom • 1 clove garlic, minced • 3 tsp. salt • 4 cups rice • water

Combine the meat and yogurt in a bowl, mix well, and let sit for half an hour. In a cup, dilute the saffron in a tablespoon of hot water. Melt a knob of the butter in a large saucepan and brown the onions until golden. Add the meat with the yogurt to the onions, along with all the spices, garlic, and salt, and sauté until the meat is browned on all sides and has formed a dark crust. Then add the rice and sauté for a few minutes. Douse with 5 cups of water, add the saffron liquid, and stir. Cover and cook until the rice and meat are tender. Serve hot.

TURKEY
Cacik

- 3 cups yogurt, drained • 2 small cucumbers, peeled and grated • extra virgin olive oil
- garlic clove, minced • fennel fronds • salt • Optional: tomatoes • Optional: red or green peppers

In a bowl, combine the yogurt with the cucumbers, oil, garlic, fennel, and salt. At this point, if desired, the tomatoes and peppers can be added to make the dish more visually attractive. Cacik generally accompanies cheeses, especially feta.

LEBANON

Labaneya

- 1 garlic clove, minced • 1 scant cup yogurt, drained • extra virgin olive oil • 1 onion, chopped
- salt • 5 cups spinach, cut into large pieces • 1 heaping cup rice • 1 leek, thinly sliced

Mix the garlic and yogurt and set aside. Heat oil in a skillet and sauté the onion with salt until golden. Add the spinach and sauté over a high flame, stirring gently. Add the rice and leek and sauté for about 2 minutes. Cover with one quart of water and bring to a boil. Reduce heat to low, stirring occasionally, until the rice is cooked. If the soup dries out too much, add hot water. Reduce heat to low, adjust seasoning with salt, and add the garlic yogurt, stirring vigorously. Serve hot, but do not let boil.

BELGIUM

Broccoletti Au Gratin with Yogurt

- 18 oz. broccoli florets • ½ cup low fat yogurt, drained
- 1 tbsp. freshly grated Parmiggiano-Reggiano • freshly ground black pepper
- 1 tbsp. whole wheat breadcrumbs • 1 tbsp. sliced almonds

Cut a cross in the end of each broccoli floret and steam for about 5 minutes or until softened. Transfer to a non-stick roasting pan, arranging close together in a single layer. Mix the yogurt and Parmiggiano-Reggiano, season with pepper, and spread over the broccoli. Then sprinkle with breadcrumbs and almonds. Cook 15 – 20 minutes in an oven preheated to 375°F.

BULGARIA

Eggs Drowned in Yogurt

• 2 tbsp. wine vinegar • salt • 8 eggs • 2 garlic cloves, smashed into a paste with salt
• 1½ cups yogurt, drained • 7 tbsp. butter • paprika

Pour 2 cups of water into a low-sided pan and add the vinegar and salt. Bring to a simmer and gently crack each egg into a cup, being careful not to break the yolks. Gently pour each egg into the water. Cover and cook for about 3 minutes, until the yolks are fully enveloped in a thin film. Now remove the cover and cook for 5 more minutes, or until cooked through. Remove the eggs with a skimmer and set aside. Repeat the operation with the four remaining eggs and arrange all of the cooked eggs on plates. In the meantime, mix the garlic into the yogurt. Arrange the yogurt mixture over the eggs. In a small saucepan, melt the butter and add the paprika. Pour this sauce over the yogurt and eggs.

ARABIA

Tahini Yogurt

• 2 garlic cloves • salt • ⅔ cup tahini (sesame paste) • ⅔ cup yogurt
• juice of 3 lemons, strained • Optional garnish: parsley

In a mortar, smash the garlic with a pinch of salt into a paste. Then mix in the tahini. A little at a time, add the yogurt and lemon juice, whisking briskly to obtain a smooth and dense mixture. Adjust seasoning with salt. Serve in a bowl and garnish with chopped parsley.

The Land of Yogurt

by Carlo Vischi

There's a place in Italy where yogurt is truly a star: the Alto Adige. We are in the province of Bolzano, where the valleys and mountains offer scenes whose common denominator is stunning beauty. While the landscape plays a fundamental role in guiding the flows of tourists toward the ski resorts in the winter and to charming and relaxing destinations during the summer, visitors to the Alto Adige will find an added bonus in the special cuisine and the setting dominated by the rearing of cattle. There are over 1,200 shepherds' huts in the Alto Adige, some converted into restaurants, but more commonly inhabited by people who choose a lifestyle connected to nature. Thanks to laws that prevent the division of grazing lands between different heirs, these shepherds have their land to farm, and their herds to raise. The cuisine is founded on the land, born poor, and fully preserves its originality, featuring broths and "canderli," which are large dumplings of bread, milk, flour, and egg, accompanied by whatever the pantry has to offer: salted and smoked ham, liver, vegetables....

The wide variety of specialties in the region's culinary tradition brings together the influences and contributions of a mild climate, profoundly different cultures, and a talent for hospitality. In this border region, the list of dishes ranges from recipes with a decidedly Austrian-Tyrolean character to masterful interpretations of classic Italian cuisine. The range of choice is vast and the surprises are pleasant, especially when they appear so naturally. For example, there is an overlap in Val Badia with Ladin cuisine, with its dishes: panicia, bales, turtres da erba, crafuns mori. Definitely not to be missed are the local cheeses, such as Alpkase, Pustra Bergkase, Tirolese, and Hoch Pustertaler, and delicacies such as chamois and roe-deer salami, and Kaminwurst and Hauswurst. Speck, a salted and smoked raw ham, is the true prince among them. Since the Middle Ages it has been common practice in the Alto Adige to de-bone, season, and age hams by hanging them from the ceiling. A tendency to smoke the hams became prevalent in the 1700s. That preservation technique gave rise to "bachen," today called speck.

Other local products include asparagus from Terlano. A beautiful white color, very tender and sweet in

flavor, it is the star ingredient of many outstanding culinary creations. First among them is Bozner Sauce, the preferred sauce in the area to accompany the asparagus.

And then there are the desserts, rich in dried fruit, honey, figs, and spices, often made using leftover bread or fresh fruit (zelten, fiadoni, pinza, and strudel).

Finally, the wines. With approximately 5,000 hectares of vineyards, the Alto Adige qualifies itself in the Italian winemaking panorama with its top quality products. Nearly 80 percent of the hills and valleys are covered with vineyards, and the leading towns are those scattered along the wine route. More than 20 varieties are produced here, based on local grapes such as the Schiava, and on the Bordeaux and Burgenlad vines planted last century.

Yogurt also plays an important role in this setting. For the past few years, the Tourist Association of Vipiteno, in collaboration with the area's hotels, has organized "Yogurt Days." Another participant is the city dairy in Vipiteno, which is carving a market share for itself with its yogurt, including an organic line.

The organizers, in drawing up the calendar of events, offer yogurt tastings in the valleys branching off from Vipiteno, with special gastronomic offers. Restaurants and hotels also participate in the initiative with special dishes based on yogurt made with locally produced milk.

The suggested wines are produced by:

Accademia dei Racemi
via Santo Stasi Primo
74024 Manduria (Ta)
Tel. 099-9711660

Arunda Vivaldi
via Civ 53
39010 Melina (Bz)
Tel. 0471-668033

Azienda agricola "Gini"
via G. Matteotti 42
37032 Monforte d'Alpone (Vr)
Tel. 045-7611908

Barone Pizzini
via Brescia 3/A
25050 Timoline
di Cortefranca (Bs)
Tel. 030-984136

Bellisario Cantina Sociale di Matelica
via A. Merloni 12
62024 Matelica (Mc)
Tel. 0737-787247

Beretta Cecilia
via Belviglieri 30
37131 Verona (Vr)
tel.045-8402111

Bodegas Gutièrrez
Colonia
Avda, de la Bajamar, 40
Cadice (Spagna)
Imported by:
Domori
piazza Borgo Pila 39
(Torre B) Genova
Tel. 010-5959888

Ca 'd Gal
via Valdivilla 108
12058 S. Stefano Belbo (At)
Tel. 0141-847103

Ca' Ronesca
via Lonzano 27
34070 Dolegna del Collio (Go)
Tel. 0481-60034

Cantina Produttori
di Cornaiano
via S. Martino, 24
39050 Cornaiano (Bz)
Tel. 047-1662403

Cantina Produttori di Terlano
via Colle d'Argento, 1
39018 Terlano (Bz)
Tel. 047-1257135

Cantina Produttori
di Valdobbiadene
via S. Giovanni, 65
S. Giovanni di Valdobbiadene (Tv)
Tel. 042-3982070

Caprai Arnaldo Val di Maggio
località Torre
06036 Montefalco (Pg)
Tel. 0742-378523

Carpené Malvolti
via Carpenè 1
31015 Conegliano (Tv)
Tel. 0438-23531

Castel de Paolis
via Val de Paolis
00046 Grottaferrata (Roma)
Tel. 06-94316025

Casetta F.lli
via Castellero 5
12040 Vezza d'Alba (Cn)
Tel. 0173-65010

Cavit
via del Ponte 31
38100 Ravina di Trento (Tn)
Tel. 0461-922055

Colterenzio Produttori
strada del Vino 8
39050 Cornaiano (Bz)
Tel. 04771-66246

Contadi Castaldi
via Colzano 32
25030 Adro (BS)
Tel. 030-7450126

Cusumano
contrada San Carlo S.S. 113
90047 Partinico (PA)
Tel. 091-8903456

D'Araprì
via Zannotti, 30
71016 San Severo (Fg)
Tel. 088-2227643

De Tarczal
via G.B. Miori, 4
38060 Marano d'Isera (Tn)
Tel. 046-4409134

Dezzani F.lli
via Pinin Giachino 142
14025 Cocconato d'Asti (At)
Tel. 0141-907044

Distil. Bonaventura Maschio
via Vizza 6
31018 Galarine (Tv)
Tel. 0434-756611

Donnafugata
via Sebastiano Lipari
91025 Marsala (Tp)
Tel. 0923-999555

Duca di Salaparuta
via Nazionale S.S. 113
90014 Casteldaccia (Pa)
Tel. 091-945201

Enrico Serafino
frazione Valpone 79
12043 Canale (Cn)
Tel. 0173-967111

Ercole Velenosi
via dei Biancospini 11
63100 Ascoli Piceno (Ap)
Tel. 0736-341218

Fabiano
via Verona 6
37060 Sona (Vr)
Tel. 045-6081111

Fattoria del Cerro Saiagricola
via Grazianella 5
53040 Acquaviva
di Montepulciano (Si)
Tel. 0578-767722

Fattoria Le Corti
via San Pietro di Sotto 1
50026 San Casciano di Val Pesa (Fi)
Tel. 055-820123

Fazi Battaglia
via Roma 117
60032 Castelpliano (An)
Tel. 0731-831444

Felluga Marco
via Gorizia 121
34072 Gradisca d'Isonzo (Go)
Tel. 0481-99164

Fontanacandida
via Fontanacandida 11
00040 Monteporzio Cat. (Rm)
Tel. 06-9420066

Francoli F.lli Cantine
Vini Distillerie
via Romagnano, 20
28074 Ghemme (No)
Tel. 0163844711

Italo Mazziotti
località Mecona Bonvino
via Cassia 10
01023 Bolsena (Vt)
Tel. 0761-799049

Lanciola
via Imprunetana 210
50023 Impruneta (Fi)
tel. 055-208324

Leopardi Dittajutti
via Marina II. 26
60026 Numana (An)
Tel. 0717390116

Livon
via Montarezza 33
frazione Dolegnano
33048 S. Giovanni al Natisone (Ud)
Tel. 0432-757173

Lungarotti
via Angeloni
06089 Torgiano (Pg)
Tel. 075-988661

Maison Ruinart Champagne
4. rue de Crayeres
Reims Cedex (France)
Distribuito da Philarmonica
Via Cefalonia 70
Cristal Palace Brescia (Bs)
Tel. 030-2279601

Marchesi di Barolo
via Alba 12
12060 Barolo (Cn)
Tel. 0173-564400

Masciarelli
via Gamberale 1
66010 Salmartino
sulla Marrucina (Ch)
Tel. 0871-85241

Mastroberardino
via Manfredi 75/81
84042 Atripalda (Av)
Tel. 0825-614111

Montresor Giacomo
ca' Di Cozzi 16
37124 Verona (Vr)
Tel. 045-913399

Nuova Agrioltura Terre dei Sesi
contrada Barone
Pantelleria
Tel. 0923-915712
Distribuito da Perlino
via Valgera 24
14100 Asti (Av)
Tel. 0141-446811

Pellegrino
via del Fante 39
91025 Marsala (Tr)
Tel. 0923-719911

Planeta
contrada Dispensa Int. 1
92013 Melfi (Ag)
Tel. 092-580009

Rivera
via S.S. 98 KM 19.800
70031 Andria (Ba)
Tel. 088-3569501

Rocca di Montegrossi
località Monti in Chianti
53016 Gaiole (Si)
Tel. 0577-747267

Russiz Superiore
località Russiz Superiore
34070 Capriva del Friuli (Go)
Tel. 0481-80328/99164

Sartori
via Casette 2
37024 S. Maria Negrar
in Valpolicella (Ve)
Tel. 0456028011

Satta Michele
località Vigna al Cavaliere
57022 Castagneto Carducci (Li)
Tel. 0565-763483

Scubla Roberto
via Rocca Bernarda 22
33040 Ipplis di Premariacco (Ud)
Tel. 0432-716258

Roberto Zeni
via Stretta 2 frazione Grumo
38010 San Michele all'Adige (Tn)
Tel. 0461-6504656

Romagnoli Cantine
via Genova 20
29020 Villò di Vigolzone (Pc)
Tel. 0523-870129

Tasca d'Almerita
viale Regione Siciliana 401
90020 Sclafani Bagni (Pa)
Tel. 091-6459711

Tenuta dell'Ornellaia
via Bolgherese 192
57020 Bolgheri (Li)
Tel. 0565-762140

Tenuta Le Fracce
via Castel del Lupo 5
località Mairano
27045 Casteggio (Pv)
Tel. 0383-82526

Tenuta Roveglia
località Roveglia 1
25010 Pozzolengo (Bs)
Tel. 030-918663

Tenuta Sette Ponti
località Oreno
31040 San Giustino Valdarno (Ar)
Tel. 055-977443

Tenute Ambrogio
e Giovanni Folonari
via de Bardi 28
50125 Firenze (Fi)
Tel. 055-200281

Terre da Vino
via Bergesia
12060 Barolo (Cn)
Tel. 0173-564611

Terre de' Trinci
via Fiamenga, 57
06034 Foligno (Pg)
Tel. 0742320165

Torraccia del Piantavigna
via Romagnano 29/a
28074 Ghemme (No)
Tel. 0163-840040

Vidussi
via Spessa 20
34070 Capriva del Friuli (Go)
Tel. 0481-80072

Villa
via Villa 12
25040 Monticelli Brusati (Bs)
Tel. 030-652329

Villa Montoggia
strada Parasio 16
17076 Ovada (Al)
Tel. 0143-822039

Zenato
via San Benedetto 8
37019 Peschiera del Garda (Vr)
Tel. 045-7550300